i

c

o

p

e

HOLLYWOOD NOTEBOOK

BY WENDY C. ORTIZ

ONE

The hands smell of cigarettes. Eyes red. Errant hairs, tendrils on the pillow. Blue pen marks on the pinky, left. An elbow in repose. Toes curled under down comforter. Grey matter tired, maybe lazy at this not so late hour. Abandoning thoughts of turning the oven on, slipping the last cut of bread inside, butter melting on its white crispy pores. Still no cold water runs in the tap. Night quiet. Tongue caressing teeth and the tobacco taste all inside. No hunger, but rather, a giving up, as if all the tasks laid out are monumentally huge and cannot be undertaken, no matter deadlines, promises or other such nonsense.

Stretching. Nipples hard. Gray cotton shirt riding over the belly. Wrists curled in writer's pose. The pose, too, of fighters for sometimes we are both.

All of the new knowledge slowly wafts by unless it can be caught hold of and respun, jagged edges alchemized into something smoother—or not—in the laboratory.

Labor being an important part of *laboratory*.

I write from a fourth floor perch. Avocado green Naugahyde loveseat, an occasional bird staring in the direction of my window from the rooftop next door. South-facing windows. A ceiling fan that gets started up around March, April, and will be in use until October if we're lucky. French press coffee. The musical car horns that parade around, announcing fruits, vegetables, and women's clothing for sale from vans ambling down Kingsley Drive.

That gummy-mouthed feeling takes hold.

It takes hold when I am speaking of something important, deep, the truth that fights to stay inside only I am pushing it out, through my mouth. Scratched vocal chords. Soreness. The speaking through dark clouds. My form becomes dense as wet wool, my words mashed and thickened until they escape my throat and pop into the air. It all takes on a thickness like suffocation, smoke so thick you must yell to be heard.

My volume never rises. There is never any fire. Just a perpetual sinking not unlike ocean depths that press against the lungs, as every word unfolds and I speak of something unspeakable, until it hits air.

TWO

Kept is such a pleasing word to me, even in its one syllable, it presents such soft tongue and quiet meeting of lips:

The Notebook on Loss::Astrological Assessments and Queries::Evidence in Favor of Anarchism::Writing Pedagogy::Dreams::Poetry Before Bed::the journal::Responses (Take My Pulse)::Notes [On Everything]

THREE

I read Hemingway, his writing about horseracing and hunger. In between, lots of sensual signposts.

He writes of spring and 'false spring.'

I get off the bus, bookmark in place. The park with the artificial lake. The smell of moss, lighter than the scummy scent of the marina in Olympia, Washington.

Hemingway wrote of fishing, the fishermen, goats, goat milk. Poverty. Sweatshirts as underwear. He writes of these things and I think of S. and I in our best clothes, dining at Musso & Frank on Hollywood Boulevard. The $100 dinners that set each of us back, stubbornly taken before the winter holidays. And I think of how there is no reason to demand cold running water in my apartment; I pay such low rent. I'm thrilled with my windows, the view of downtown, the proximity of palm treetops. I am fond of the light blue carpets and black and white tiled bathroom, the 60s era refrigerator and the Formica table. I have no fireplace to roast chestnuts or throw mandarin peels. I have impeccable bowls, made by friends.

FOUR

I learned how to play chess in third grade. The shapes of each piece, the various directions they could make on the board, the divisions between those who could play chess and those who could not fascinated me, so much so that it was a mystery every time I sat down to play.

As I got older, my game became sloppy. At twenty I was sitting in the picture window of a Thai restaurant in Hollywood playing chess with a lover at one a.m., pushing the game along so that we could go home and fuck some more.

Sex as a teenager often felt like chess. I had learned at a young age; it sometimes set me apart from my peers. I could tease an aggressive move from my opponent with the naive-appearing move of a soft, open pawn. I could set up a small window of opportunity where my opponent might try to penetrate then close it up with cold-hearted maneuvering of a rook or bishop. My knight could do a little dance in the corner, lulling my opponent into its careful, plotted steps while I watched my other pieces with fear for their safety. Or I could push each piece to the forefront of a game whose end was my only intention, playing half-consciously and completely open to risk.

As a child, each icon of the chessboard held stories within its design. I loved the way the bishop resembled a stone flame. The queen had hips under her dress. The pawns had names, and their sacrifice was noble. My rooks were heavies, sent in to assign power, do my dirty work, while some maiden lived in each piece's windowless confines, soberly dictating the direction of her castle-in-motion. I enjoyed the feel of each piece in my hand, the texture of wood or marble pieces, an eyeless horse, a bishop with a nub at its top, the tiny pointed crown of a queen and the cross adorning the top of the king.

By fifteen, my body felt newly textured, a container of stories which were written and rewritten daily. I could exude a pawn quality, the opening to pieces of more importance, more weight, but the first to be sacrificed. I could become the fickle knight that pranced in corners, retracing steps, caught in confusions. My body could mow down a conquest like the rook, but with the shy, martyr character of the pawn. I could be the queen, hidden behind a garden of characters, waiting for consummation, or just to be overthrown.

FIVE

A respite from the men who ogle, whisper, brush up against, expose themselves: yesterday as I walked to the bus stop, the man who pushes his shopping cart up and down Kingsley talking loudly in mixtures of English and Spanish with exotic glossolalia thrown in, stopped in the middle of the sidewalk and directed his gaze at me.

He said that he had saved this snake from a crow (it was more an announcement, to the neighborhood, even though his eyes were on me), and my eyes traveled down his arm to his hand, where his dark brown fingers lightly pinched the head of a thin black snake that was halfway out of a crumpled paper bag, amidst clothes and plastic bottles and other similar treasures. I expressed my admiration.

We parted. I thought about him all day.

SIX

It has become friend and enemy. The black cat running beside me. The echo that won't leave the tunnel, that follows me outside. Heavy breath in the dark room even when I'm alone, the tears that run into the corners of the mouth and the ones that run down the neck, the dead branches of palm trees that need to be shorn.

Loss.

I want to wear out the subject.

◆

Did I tell you? I spent the last evening of my twenties on the roof of my apartment, watching the lunar eclipse. It was warm and still I wore my lavender shawl. The roof held all the heat of the day. The moon was just an outline with a red shadow over her mass. I held my knees. That red eye watched me right back.

Later, I watched from the Naugahyde loveseat the sliver turn wider, wider, until it was the utmost silver, the pearl, the advent, for me, of a new decade. As irrelevant the concept of time is, I made it relevant that night. Or the full moon did.

SEVEN

When I told Bernard Cooper where I'm living now, an apartment in Hollywood, the name of the street, he exclaimed "I grew up around there!"

It was only after picking up a photography book in a bookstore that seemed to laser-focus on Charles Bukowski that I remembered I'm in his old neighborhood, I walk the same streets, have gone into the corner sex shop he frequented. It was only after rereading *The White Album* by Joan Didion that I remembered her tales of life in Hollywood, in which she mentions "the Franklin Avenue house," and I scan my mind for the neighborhood she describes, wondering at my proximity to it. I'm near the vortex they all once inhabited.

EIGHT

I go through periods where my writing feels like a deep place I want to go to again and again, like a new lover whose first name I know, never asking about the last. I remember writing in the attic, hours on end, swooning with the need, and when the room became too cold to continue, the mourning: *I will have to leave you until tomorrow. I can't wait to see you again.*

It is not a ritual for me. It is not a wet place. It's like walking around the lip of a volcano, my body humming with the danger, and its beauty makes me just want to step inside. When it's not that, it's the shadow next to me, lightly pressing its finger to my lips; when it's not that, it's the shock of a lover I think I know everything about, until s/he brings out the instruments from the box under the bed...and I want to know this experience again and again.

Which brings me here.

NINE

I finished trying on the umpteenth pair of vintage eyeglass frames and walked back out into the heat towards the hospital. A woman stopped me. I'd noticed her earlier mostly because she seemed lost in thought, and her yellow t-shirt announced in spangly old glitter iron-on MOZART. She looked out of place at Vermont and Barnsdall simply because she looked so lucid. The rest of us seemed to drift around her like whirlpools of air on the sidewalks.

She said, "I'm conducting research on the imagination." She looked out at the parking lot. We were standing in front of Jon's Grocery.

"Can you imagine a tree standing in the middle of this parking lot?" she asked. I looked out at the blacktop teeming with parked cars, some moving like sharks. "Yeah," I said. I can imagine pretty much anything.

"What kind of tree would be best here?" she inquired.

I thought for a second. "Well, it depends," I heard myself say. "It depends on whether we're talking 'best here' for me, or for these cars, or for the community..."

She agreed that this might be the case, it was circumstantial in a way. She seemed pleased. The skin on her face was tight but crinkling in all the smile parts, and her gray hair was straight and bluntly cut one length. She held a small clipboard with her notes.

"So what kind of tree could you imagine?" she asked me. We kept looking at the parking lot. I told her what kind.

She smiled and nodded. "Would you be able to smell it?" she asked finally. I stopped and tried, and after a moment told her I knew I could if I wasn't thinking of so many other things and where I had to be. I wanted to tell her about how as I child I could make the sounds of the Hollywood Freeway turn into ocean waves, but there was no time. I looked towards the hospital and she released me from her grasp.

TEN

I've been languishing in the prose of *Finding A Form* (W. Gass) and yesterday welcomed the arrival of J. Berger's *The Shape of A Pocket*, which I intend to begin this week. The time spent with friends threatens the time I spend with books. The music playing in the background threatens my white walls, which friends are always gently admonishing me to paint or decorate with something other than white. I prefer the white, the big empty, and like to accent it with black, and cornflower blue. If not this, then the rooftop is my next favorite place, palm trees gently swinging, two bottles of red wine, a candle, a blanket with friends seated all around, far away from the white walls and the books, underneath stars and blue-black sky.

With the ceiling fan whipping the air and passionflower tea in the fridge, I believe we have finally hit summer.

My life since I've moved back to Los Angeles has felt like traversing a rocky path of milestones that double as landmines. Landmines because once I hit the milestone there is an explosion of emotion, either fueled by the notebooks I write in and what seeps out into them, or fueled by red wine or pale ale, or just the throwaway words of a friend who meant better but the sentiments came out all wrong.

The latest landmine/milestone: The CD I bought last summer in a subconscious fit of nostalgia, The Reindeer Section's *Y'All Get Scared Now, Ya Hear!*, has finally been snatched up from me by a buyer in, of all places, Yakima, Washington. Yakima, where P. and I once drove through on a roadtrip with no maps, no itinerary. Washington, where I bought the CD in the first place.

I listened to the first two songs, thought of Sh., how he played it once when we were in his apartment, or excerpts of it, wondered if I had heard it in his black car as well, and then the landmine exploded and I could never repeat listening to it again.

I will listen to it before mailing it to Yakima. Milestone.

ELEVEN

I have lived in three residences my entire life.

I had four addresses, but in only three structures.

Ratner Street, Adams Street Southeast, North Kingsley Drive. On Adams I moved upstairs from the downstairs and swore I would never pay more than $200 rent, ever. The highest it ever got was $202.50.

On Kingsley I pay three times that, and I live alone. I looked at an apartment last night just four blocks from mine that included a parking space, but decided I could not bear to give up my rooftop access (with its access to stars, planets, and views of the city) or my big windows that overlook the smaller apartments nearby, or the fact that I live so far back from the street, which is also wide enough to accommodate at least three cars driving side by side. While I liked the idea of living on North Serrano Street, I decided to remain rooted. Again.

TWELVE

I don't know what I want or what I'm doing.
FALSE.
I do know what I want but not sure what I'm doing.
HALF-TRUTH.
I don't have my ideas lined up straight / I'm overwhelmed / Mars in Pisces holds me back / the fighter fish underwater, hiding behind a rock.
Pissed. Grumpy. Fat. Bitchy.
Yeah, well, fuck you.
TRUTH.

THIRTEEN

I'm a writer like so many other unknown writers all over this city. I have ordinary concerns, like paying rent on an apartment in Hollywood, the merry-go-round of moving my car twice a week for street cleaning, riding the Metro five days out of seven to a job, wondering about love and obsessing about sex and publishing and what will happen next.

I look, glance, really, at the windows of the apartment next door. I have seen a woman lying on what I originally thought was a desk, it's so often strewn with books or papers or even implements like scissors, but it turned out to be a bed. I realized this when I saw her in white underwear, doing leg exercises, staring out at something in the room that I couldn't see.

There is no curtain on my kitchen window, not even a shade. Across the way is the deserted rooftop of the apartment next door. One window over from the busy bed of the leg-exercising woman is a man who has a quilt and a computer and one more window over I can see his shower. I am careful to avert my gaze, especially when I hear sounds like a waterfall.

The helicopters are sky piranha. They interrupt and seize the air. They fly rude and illogical ovals, sometimes sport spotlights, and I would like to know what story they are following. If I lie in my great big bathtub and they enter the space of my window, I worry passively at what they can see. I suppose I am to believe they are beyond peeping and that their purposes are more important and respectable.

I pull the plug and let the sudsy water drain out.

I'm not even here, in Hollywood, to act or write screenplays. I left Olympia, Washington, its own kind of incubator, but before that I left North Hollywood, where I spent most of my life, the place that would be more specific and recognizable if I called it Sun Valley Adjacent or just Panorama City.

I mostly ignore the white wine, cold, at the bottom of the refrigerator. The cigarettes call to me from time to time these days, twice in a twenty-four hour period. Sometimes I reach out to them a third, fourth time.

Because I'm a writer and have this job that's about not-writing, I take a sick day, fortunately paid, and use it to write.

But there's never really a finish. Instead there is a pause, and in that pause, I sigh a lot, or I pick up a new book, or page through a magazine, pluck my eyebrows, glare at helicopters while supine on my Naugahyde loveseat. I admonish myself for sitting too much, for how much time I've spent inside for so many hours, but then pat myself on the back for how many pages were produced, regardless that right now they have no destination. No endpoint.

The helicopter cuts wider and wider swaths in the air, circles like the hunter that it is, and we are helpless in our apartments at this madness.

FOURTEEN

My body remembered yesterday how much it loves the ocean; the roll and tumble, the suspense of a solid set coming towards us; the weightlessness, as another mermaid pulled me along and I remembered what it was like to be five years old with her; the water so cold it transmits an ache to the feet until I just glide on in and my entire body is submerged; the second plunge under a wave we don't have enough time to ride; the friendly swells that lift and fall underneath me; the slap of water to the head, the ocean reminding me who's in charge—

Beautiful, to have spent much of the day with M., and the presence of her father who's also known me since I was under four feet tall, and the ocean, who's known me forever.

FIFTEEN

I read at World Stage in Leimert Park. I drank two beers with S. and S. in a bar around the corner beforehand. I felt my voice go sing-songy as I read, with the cadence I wrote the piece in, with the nuances of the parentheses and brackets guiding me around in little labyrinths, which was just the effect I wanted.

It was the piece I was most frightened to read, the one I almost cut at the last second, and it was the piece that people came up to me afterwards to comment on: 'intense', 'powerful' they said.

I swooned.

I was glad such comments could come from a reckless endeavor as to try and document such a complex and sorrowful state of events. Pain turned into pleasure.

SIXTEEN

And if you're the type of person who likes to sit with your pain and work it, knead it into a ball you can throw, more power to you.

And if you're the type of person who hates to sit with your pain and wants to throw it out the window in its unkneadedness, its messy sticky goo state, I want to give you a compass to lead you back to where the pain came from.

And if you prefer to drink too many beers in Elysian Park then take two hits off a joint and beg your party date to keep talking as he drives you home so you have something to concentrate on, then barely make it upstairs where you'll puke three times then maybe just maybe be able to come despite all the booze and drugs loaded up in your blood, well,

I call you sister, twin.

SEVENTEEN

The sense of rushing around and only living to get somewhere else : sleep coming in the form of six minute increments between presses of the snooze button : calling taxis so as not to waste time driving, parking : calling the Indian restaurant on Vermont, the Thai restaurant on Hollywood Blvd. for delivery of food in order to have time to read and write : stops at the library but never for long; no browsing : lacking pauses, I move smoothly from metro subway to metro bus on the best days : the anger that heats my fingertips when I feel I am being cheated of precious time : the unconsciousness of too much beer, too many tokes of a handmade joint and a Saturday night that is wasted on more than one level : remembering to stop and stare : remembering to breathe deep, watch the palm trees, remember the swaying motion of the waves and their relation to the sway of these palm fronds.

EIGHTEEN

Irrational and unobservant, two words that people used to describe me when I was a teenager. 'Irrational' came from the friend I held hands with and danced with and who made me pad thai with ketchup; 'unobservant' came from the brother of a boyfriend, someone not considered, by many, to be a wholly reliable source.

Nevertheless.

I've held onto these two words for many years and tried to glean their meanings. More often, I've wondered about the people who gave me these labels. And most recently, I have taken a guess as to what they were talking about.

Irrational: I puff up sometimes at the slightest provocation. I relish debates and challenges with the right opponents—some I will just walk away from, having established, silently, that the subject—not the person—is not worth the time or effort. I sometimes make connections among things other people can't see. I sometimes lapse into rationalizations that are simply, irrational.

Unobservant: I walk around, not in a daze so much as a web that keeps me separate. You may not get my full attention. I'm listening to much more than what everyone can hear, often. I sometimes don't notice external shifts because I'm paying deep attention to internal ones, invisible ones that others are responding to without knowing, others who are instead pointing out that the book's been moved, or the street name has changed.

I try to be engaged but often there's a story behind my eyes that is whipping around like a hurricane trying to keep my attention.

NINETEEN

Tossed, bandied about, in a day of books and magazines. I descend to the subway platform carrying the unabridged journal of Sylvia Plath, flipping pages, skimming, staying with entries lyrical and ironic and also searching; I'm even a little self-conscious about the hunger I exhibit in reading it.

I'm interested in what was being published as fact by *Reader's Digest* in the 1970s (not to mention what was considered 'strange') and my other interest is in locating some of the stories I mulled over as a kid, having to do with unexplainable nonhuman footprints crossing small towns, ghosts and the houses they lived in, crop circles.

TWENTY

a treesit : selling everything and finally getting the van and
moving to Mexico : selling everything except the laptop and
cell phone and some clothes and all my writerly paraphernalia,
enough to fit into a small bag : flying to Spain, then going to
Basqueland : writing every day for hours upon hours : living on
a boat, summer, in the East Bay Marina, Olympia, Washington :
staying with A. in Philly for however long she'll let me : extended
road trip across the country : Spanish everyday : swimming in
the ocean everyday : cooking classes : recording the stories of
my parents and my grandmother : Tulare and Visalia : Arkansas
and Ohio : studies of coral reefs, deep sea creatures, astrology,
dreams, Jung, Deleuze and Guattari, art history, Baudrillard,
Michael Ondaatje, photography and on and on and on, the
list grows hourly : stripping away everything inconsequential,
everything that will not really matter and will not impact me
deeply : this list is neverending, hence, *limitless*

TWENTY-ONE

From Sylvia Plath's unabridged journals (right to my bloodstream):

"...I fear oppressive and crushing forces, if I do not plot and manage and manipulate my path, joining: academic, creative & writing, and emotional & living & loving: writing makes me a small god: I re-create the flux and smash of the world through the small ordered word-patterns I make. I have powerful physical, intellectual and emotional forces which must have outlets, creative, or they turn to destruction and waste..."

(see: my natal astrological chart. see: Pluto in Midheaven, Mars below. see: Sun and Mercury in 5th house. see: Scorpio moon. see: born on full moon. see: all evidence fall like a house of cards then build up again, a house of cards in reverse.)

TWENTY-TWO

A boy named Chronotope handed me a photocopied and stapled article from a 1998 issue of *Race Traitor* entitled "Women and the Surrealist Revolution." Thank you, Chronotope.

In this interview, Penelope Rosemont reminds me of why I am here: because I like field theories 'in which poetry, art, revolutionary politics, psychoanalysis (!), alchemy, and the influences of different cultures mix together in totally new ways." [(*!*) *mine*]

There are myriad ways to express this and intricate, limitless ways of living this. I find myself at square one, again. And I am thankful for the subtle reminder.

TWENTY-THREE

Eighty degrees, sun, sweat pouring down my back while standing in the bowels of the metro station—and still, I feel the season changing. The sun falls earlier in the sky. The wind in Ventura last weekend had a scent I recognized as autumn, the kind we get, Southern California autumn.

I let decisions steep all summer before unleashing them. October, November—these are often the months the changes are born. I wish I could skip September altogether.

blood lake. volcanic upswing. the colors of Georgia O'Keefe. The quarter moon, new just a few nights ago...the despair that Ted Hughes destroyed the journal entries Sylvia wrote just three days before her suicide...

keening

living in Big Sur. Or Mexico.

The woman next to me drinking tomato juice on ice, freckled arms and face, softly stroking her forearm, close, so close to my light blue angora-covered arm.

Fell asleep I think before the plane even took off. As we taxied down the runway. Then woke myself up with a violent start—I'd begun a dream, I grunted, loud, pulsed, started, embarrassed, then shifted in my seat, settled back in but not as relaxed as before.

Plath writing of dreams and Jung and reading Bishop, Pound, rejections by major publishers, acceptances in the *New Yorker*.

The feeling of not accepting anything—as though I will not accept what other people—normal?—will accept...

The possibility that melancholy has any 'charge' to it at all—or if it is the opposite...

TWENTY-FOUR

Struggling with wanting to throw all my belongings into a bag. Dreading going back to work. Hating the dread. The ones with forty-hour work week lives that feel quaint, afforded them the ability to live independently as they also did their art FUCK I guess I'm doing that. This is what I have. This is how I'll make do.

I still have a life force even when I feel the death force riding me.

TWENTY-FIVE

notebooks::good traveling vehicle (old jeep,
preferably)::camera::slide film::polaroid::pens I can
trust::binders::laptop::cell phone::good shoes (one pair
for hiking and running/the other for good restaurants)::a
good travel bag::costumes for every occasion::one
hat::sunglasses::press pass::digital voice recorder::old
fashioned tape recorder::clothes that don't require
ironing::money::calendar/date book::a thick, sturdy
address book::coffee beans::French press::some cigarettes
(menthol)::access to a bathtub

TWENTY-SIX

Johnny Cash has died.

Was it "At San Quentin" or "At Folsom Prison"?—my memory fails me. One or the other or both, my father kept these albums in the patio by the record player. One or the other was played when the amber liquid in his bottle was nearly gone.

My grandmother was also known to have liked a little Johnny Cash in her time.

We will spend at least $5 this weekend playing his music, as S. said, "in a gritty bar with people not possessed by the giddiness of bourgeois excess but who somehow carve out a little space against the cruelties of the world."

I will miss his beautiful shadow.

I underestimated my grandmother's love of Johnny Cash.

When I visited her she told me he was the greatest guitar player ever, that she has always loved him and knew he was sick and that she hadn't known that June died.

My grandmother will be 88 in two months.

We played a set of 7 at Tee Gee's last night, but it was interrupted a couple of times with random jukebox selections, not bad, but still...luckily the 7th song played just as the giddiness of bourgeois excess took over the room...

TWENTY-SEVEN

The last day of summer: hot. I lounged in a chair in the beautiful backyard of Tropico Nopal, an art gallery at Beverly and Union. We checked out artist lofts as though we were in the market, and wrote with the kids and I watched as they did theater exercises with the illustrious Omar and I wrote and wrote. Lists and lists. I let the sun beat down on my face and right arm (protecting the tattoo on the left arm) and said goodbye to summer.

At the end of our workshop, Omar had the kids do an exercise where they felt each other's pulse while sitting in a circle. I joined them. Two people felt for my pulse, and it was an interesting feeling, them searching for the sound, the beat that keeps me alive in front of them.

After, we wandered the gallery in amazement, and I had a number of long, drawn-out, fascinating conversations with artists about what they're doing, who they're doing it with, what they're excited by. All of this, with a view of downtown Los Angeles.

Lastly, a Griffith Park hike at sunset. The perfect farewell to summer.

TWENTY-EIGHT

AQ brought me amazing books about Pluto. She is sympathetic to my Pluto transit, which can be described as long, arduous, and dark. I'm recognizing that my penchant for getting rid of ten items per day is quite Plutonian—meaning I'm perhaps working this Pluto transit gracefully, in this instance—and last night I stayed up late reading among the three books, contemplating the Sun, Venus, and Mars aspects I have to Pluto.

◆

S. and I are in something like a clubhouse.

We bring in our five pack of Negro Modelo and set it on the industrial green carpet. Flyers of political and musical persuasion compete for nearly every inch of wallspace.

I like that I can smoke in here.

I ask for an ashtray and S./Boy Howdy (hereafter referred to as BH) locates one from a desk filled with audio equipment. It is the same gold glass ashtray my mother has, has had since I was a tiny kid.

This is where I become Rider Mae. The studio reminds me of my own days as a dj, at KAOS radio in Olympia, Washington. I had a solo show for one year, and now, it's everything BH can do to make me say ten words on the air.

"Air"—this is an internet radio station.

This place, thick with record albums, compact discs, wires, fans, mikes, newspapers, flyers, is the perfect place to empty out the contents of your pockets.

I am reminded that I used to date musicians habitually, and I recently broke that cycle, unpurposely.

Eating burritos across the street after the show, ten o'clock at night, I'm also reminded that this kind of thing was a daily event for me—the stacks of music, the freeform folks walking in and out, the empty pockets and piles of ephemera, the loud music, the late-evening dinner after two beers on an empty stomach. And I miss it.

TWENTY-NINE

Another night of drinking, back at Ye Rustic. Taking in the World Series in a very dark bar, fake cobwebs strung up that look like they belong there year-round. We did not have the company of the jukebox; the bartenders humored the sports fans and turned up the volume on the game.

Jack on the rocks. Beers: three? Two? More than I would usually consume on a weeknight, normally. This is not a normal week. My lover leaves the country tomorrow.

•

It was a little after 10pm on Friday. S. and I made our way down 3rd Street toward the Escape Room. We were walking, talking, holding hands then not, noticing the usual helicopters with spotlights overhead, ambulances and fire trucks barreling down the street.

When we got to Normandie, yellow caution tape and a police officer held us back. The bar was within a block from where we stood, but suddenly the gravity of the situation made it seem miles away. As soon as the cop told us to move back behind the building, someone yelled *Wendy!* and Sarah and Andy were motioning us over to their car. *Wanna get in?* Andy asked, and we scurried in before Sarah had to merge into the left lane to get us out of the developing traffic jam, avoiding the flares, cop cars, caution tape.

S. and I laughed in the backseat, thinking of how we had been walking and talking blissfully unaware into a scene of warfare.

"We were just casually strolling into the apocalypse," I said, laughing.

We made it to the next bar and successfully rerouted Chris and Ann by cell phone to our new destination. Two minutes upon arriving at the dark bar, a couple of men playing pool began yelling at each other, throwing punches. After some people stood in their way, keeping them from each other, they both stormed out. A small crowd of barflies followed. Then the sound of punches against skin. Smacking sounds against pavement. Chris and Ann had walked up to the front door, held the handle, when suddenly two men fell out onto the sidewalk, at blows.

Normandie was still blocked off by flares at 2am. We knew we would never read about it in the paper or see it on the news.

When we drove up to S's apartment a car was on fire in the middle of the street. A moment of low-grade panic swept through me. Men wielding fire extinguishers surrounded the car, put the fire out to the sound of applause from the bystanders. Fire engines noisily clambered down the street five minutes later.

An explosion could have already occurred by then.

Fire engines. As if they create the fires, not put them out. Like fire, on the move.

THIRTY

The air has me feeling asthmatic, which I'm not.

Smoking a cigarette by the window feels supremely unhealthy, considering the warning to close doors, use air conditioning (as if we all enjoy the luxury of AC) and limit outdoor activities. The ash falling from the cigarette suddenly takes on a completely different tone as it stains my black pants, smears grey, smudges. My voice is breathy, bordering on a low rasp, like when I'm recovering from a sore throat. It feels like we are in a high altitude, when really it's just fire, fire everywhere.

◆

I wonder, most of the time, if I am fundamentally hard-wired to resist monogamy. And then I wonder who is hard-wired to be monogamous. Or, if no one is hard-wired—which I would tend to believe in most cases, in most circumstances, of anything—then how will I reconcile this seeming character flaw of mine? Accountability is mine; it always has been. In this new decade beginning, for me, with the number 3, I wonder if I need to change the question, or accept that there is no answer.

THIRTY-ONE

The photos were clipped in a kind of tree until I took them down today. Little metal branches held each photograph, splayed out, the whole piece resembling a fan of color and gloss. Here is Mitla in the sun; the shadowed inner hallways of the first pension I stayed at; the grounds of the Mexico City palace; a church; the hills above Guanajuato; the green foliage of the outdoor courtyard of the motel in Oaxaca. All the photos have a hot sun quality about them.

These are some of the photographs I put up when I first moved into the apartment two years ago. I wanted to remind myself I could be alone. I had arrived alone in Mexico, negotiated my way from Mexico City to Guanajuato alone upon my arrival, even while the most difficult (poignant?) task of my first day there was to go out into the street mercados and secure a bottle opener for the two beers I'd bought myself to drink in the privacy of my small room. Alone.

They have nearly—but not completely—ceased reminding me of that time and what that time might mean to me now. I am in none of these photos. They've become flat, though still colorful in their telling.

◆

Last week, I received a package from someone whom I consider one of my best friends. She's the person who sparks my fuses, serves as a mentor and also a partner-in-crime, and whom I think of almost as much as chocolate. Plus she's a spitfire extraordinaire (and I always love those).

The package, besides containing gorgeous, engaging, and mysterious collages (dark and light, all at once) also contained two notebooks.

One is light blue and heavy. Small and thick. Like a good book. I have not even created a purpose for it but find myself wanting to carry it around with me. It also contains the giver's handwriting and this is priceless.

The second looks naughty with its black and red clothes and its svelte-ness. Again, I have not created a purpose for it, but am trying to decide between smut or political thought.

•

Random events of the last several days—

—tried not to watch the woman next door who has her blinds open as always, her bed a mess of books and notebooks, much like my living room, her unclothed limbs stretched out as she reads, unaware of my vantage point,

—purchased a glue pen and was talked into also buying a metallic gray Sharpie by a man working at the art supply store, who with every interaction, managed to touch my fingers,

—watched the Michael Jackson interview, THE one, and later that day felt as though I'd dreamt it, that I'd seen him walking through Las Vegas buying things left and right, his children in masks, his baby under a veil,

—organized all the notebooks on a shelf in front of where I work most, (in this order [smallest to largest]: books to read; more books to read + notes; uninitiated notebook; landscapes; secret want-to-buy-things book; gift from K. book; astrology; art; terrorism; notes on Diane Arbus and other artists plus astrological musings; abortion notes + the artist Robert Williams's address, written in his own handwriting; poetry; two composition books of miscellaneous material; the book of Loss; empty grid pages; recent work; sketches; novella material; and lastly, the largest, Black n' Red, also uninitiated, from K.)

—tamales for breakfast, two days in a row,

—practically counting minutes until my lover returns to this country, all the while reading *Against Love* and enjoying the hell out of it, happy as though someone has finally written my perspective...

THIRTY-TWO

Payday to payday, the loss of an expensive lip gloss. Purposely oversleeping, my perennial ambivalence. Pissed and drunk, or buzzed and serious.

I lose my driver's license, my form of identification in a bar. How I want to leave my identity behind. *How to Disappear Completely* is my soundtrack.

Wanting a certain kind of pain to break me open, the kind where I'm dumped. Wanting it because I deserve it because I fuck around.

But he won't give me the kind of pain I want.

THIRTY-THREE

Swarm, swamped.

The days are like the buzzing of bees. I'm a swarm myself, moving, changing shape, into and out of each day. I have the potential to sting and do not. When I get to the hive again, it's time to focus, home in on the most important tasks without letting my concentration waver, and yet the Queen is still not satisfied.

•

Stop. Close your eyes. Remember the heat? Now go back to whatever you were doing.

I remember the days of rain and more rain. Wishing I could be dry as a bone. Instead, I was perpetually soaked, or at least, damp.

Then there were the dark, dry days of the sauna. Anya and I would go together. The sauna was like a huge log cabin inside a concrete gym. The only other sauna I had been to was its exact opposite: very bright, only large enough for maybe three bodies sitting close. In the log cabin sauna there was enough room to lie down, stretch, and I could be nowhere near the disembodied voice of Anya. The inflections of her voice reverberated in the gentlest way in this, our cave. I caressed my hip bone and listened, arranged my hair and listened, sat up, rubbed a calf, put both hands to my face to feel the warmth and listened.

THIRTY-FOUR

Cannibals exist, now, always. Is it cliché to hear them say they merely want to take communion? Will it make a difference if they take flesh, or organs? Is the flesh disguised in garlic, pepper, salt, because it truly needs it, or are these maskings of gastronomy, embellishments of a true cook?

To consent to be eaten: face flushed. The moment when one realizes they stand before their executioners, innocent (or are they paying for some secret guilt that will be forever concealed). The groin. Wanting to be savored, supped by another soul.

Where do we connect with these creatures? We only consider, I think, the disconnect. The to-be-eaten arriving at the door, knowing he was moving into the unknown (the way we all do, every day, only we pretend otherwise). Wishing for his body to be split, sundered, tasted, the attention one takes, makes, when cooking, the attention of the cook to what is frying, boiling, baking, and the moment when the lips meet the 'creation'—in this case, the utmost creation? one like ourselves? our mirror?, and it is here that I have a glimmer of understanding, beyond the rational (*this is what they do in some churches, metaphorically*), beyond the logical (*what life events led up to this turn of events, for both parties?*), why the cannibal believes he is eating a piece of god.

(S.: "I try to imagine the mind of such a person. Each time I draw a blank.")

THIRTY-FIVE

When I want to rip at seams I look down and see I'm standing in a bloody lake of muck.

I wear tights which are really stockings which in reality are pantyhose and I want to rip them the fuck off.

Work. Dressy. Girly.

My pantyhose make me slip in the blood muck even as I insist that I like this life I agree to go where he wants to go and agree to the hours that keep me running and the writing sits abandoned in a corner like a mute tortured child waiting to be noticed.

I will learn then to swim in the muck. Come close but be on guard—I make a mess when I think I'm drowning. Which is often.

THIRTY-SIX

It's as if a week has been lost.

A few of the days were lost in travel, driving across deserts, night and day, and one of the days was misplaced drinking golden beer in the sun, gulf-side.

The laptop perched on my pajama'd knee, thermal shirt not completely doing its job, I write among a pile of books weeded from the shelves, on their way to the thrift store donation door or to loved ones who appreciate such gifts. The sun seems far, far away; winter closes in, tries to seep into the broken window I've sealed with a padded envelope that's traveled from Prague, and there is still a week left where I can sit in pajamas and stare out the window (or do much, much more, trying to keep warm all the while).

Last night reminded me of all the nights of two years ago, sitting in overly-dark bars, putting chewed-up-looking dollars in the jukebox, struggling to remember what song I just chose as I try to choose the next, the clinking ice in the glass tumbler of Jack, the skunky Coronas and the abandoned lime wedges, the slide into an easy wave of talk, my voice going lower, my eyes adjusting to the darkness, feeling like I want my hand around a few more glass necks but knowing it's a school night and I must abstain, the glory of friendly bartenders and friends who will meet me at seedy locations and spend a few hours in my company and even drive me home...

THIRTY-SEVEN

Sometimes I hate all the connections—I want to sever all the tendrils that have reached out from me, to me—

Listening to a tape made in Prague by a friend, his ambient loft noise, and suddenly a Black Sabbath song plays—softly—it's not even foreground—and I hate him for including that song—because it reminds me of driving the roads in Olympia, Washington, the roads out to unknown farms and to reservations, and the roads that lead back to downtown, to my home of eight years, and the boy I loved there, his cool, rough hands, his pale skin and freckled arms, and his beautiful teeth and brilliance, his mind a mystery, as it still is to me, now—

But how could my friend in Prague have known this. I imagine destroying this evidence of connection he could not have known or guessed at, removing the tape and unfurling all the skein of it until it's a metallic mess of veins on the floor—

THIRTY-EIGHT

I haven't had the answers for the last two years and three months.

For some reason, I thought I had the answers before that. I could plan and the plans I made would happen, with few upsets.

Now, this is not true.

I haven't known for the last two years what I might be doing a few hours from any particular moment. Today I can barely make a plan for tomorrow. I have started to look on this not as something limiting but as something terribly exciting, sometimes just *terrible* and *exciting*.

I know very few things. I'm thirty and there are only a handful of things I can say I wholeheartedly count on.

If I told you some of them, you would see my cynical heart, the jaded, jagged edges of me. Then, too, you might also be warmed by the other—few—things I know I can count on. Much of this space has been recounting of those things, as well as much more on what I do not know, what I can't count on.

◆

Love changes from hour to hour. Not the love itself but the quality and texture of it. The continuum between love and hate has never been clearer.

Anniversaries are not always happy ones. Anniversaries themselves, happy ones, are hard to come by.

I am excited by the kind of changes that accompany earthquakes, volcanoes, power outages, and births in unexpected environs. I understand what kind of capacity I have for extreme situations and I know a little bit more about the thresholds I've touched, transgressed, built up in myself. Crying in bathtubs is beautiful. Running down trails crying and sweating even more beautiful. I fall in love with a friend over coffee and go home to the one I am in love with, who smiles at my flaws, pets me incessantly. I dream, rip seams, start over, try not to linger on wounds too long.

Sometimes I sit down in the wound and languish in the muck, the little bloody lakes of it, and then you will not hear from me for a while. All of this, I know and do not know, in the same instance. It attracts me to this life.

THIRTY-NINE

When I talk to L. about my dreams, she offers her perspective, always, that all the characters in our dreams are really parts of us.

I can go with this. I've been thinking of my recurring dreams about houses full of cats, though, and wonder what that's about (though most dream dictionaries will first reference cats as denoting sexuality)—but most recently, I've wondered about the dreams where I am either the lover or soon-to-be spouse of a major politician.

It's made me wonder about these 'parts.' I'm quite aware of some of the other 'parts'—the one who makes my eyes shine wildly and flirt shamelessly with a stranger when I'm in a monogamous relationship, or the one who pouts openly and practically stomps her feet when she doesn't get her way, for example—but what about the parts that are like a politician? Someone who has a particular kind of power?

If I delved more deeply into this, I might come up with my own resistances to politicians and the type of power they stand for—but in these dreams, there is an altogether different feeling, tone.

In the clandestine lover dream, I am thrilled to meet him in the street, and completely saddened when I have to pull away. Am I coming together with some type of power that is not mine, then relinquishing it immediately?

In the more recent dream, I am cool, complacent, and, with a straight face, contemplating marrying a Republican. In the dream I am confronted with characters who actually ask me what I'm doing because they know me, and know that, to me, this would be marriage into something I am 150% in opposition to, as I have been all of my political life (but, for the record, I'm not a Democrat, either. Far from it).

So who is this stand-in for me?

The particular politician I am set to marry (once again, I am the other woman, but won't be for long—) is someone who, on a conscious level, I see as lots of bombast, smoke & mirrors, nonsensical plastic...well, I could go on, but won't. My point is, does this dream signify a meeting with that part of myself? Do I meet that part (if it is a part) with complacence, with quiet resignation, submissively? Or is it "just" a marker for power in general—once again, a dream where I am about to enter into a contract with a powerful force?

◆

The fun seems like it's sort of dripping down and away, like when you try to catch wine drops from coming down the side of the glass onto your white pants.

Grandmothers do things like go in and out of hospitals, and entertain you while they're at it: —*Look, see that little dog in the corner?* (it's a metal wheel) —*That little bird! It's moving away from us!* (it's the dangling IV cord) —*I see a fish.* (it's a small bandage, limp and lifeless on the floor).

Besides the grandmothers and their daughters, there are also all the notebooks sitting expectantly on the shelf. They're lopsided with grief. They sigh and mutter low moans when I reach instead for a yellow legal pad from a basket that contains ancient writings, from when I was in my early 20s. A whole new story begins but dampens with every page. I prefer to look out the window. I wish I could see the birds that like to surf the palm fronds. Where are they?

Soon my closest friend in L.A. will move about 300 miles away. That pains me. Her and her thousand pieces of food. Away.

I feel tender like new skin and yet I rumble with threat, thunder bellowing underneath all the conversation. All at once I feel meek and mewing. I must wait here. The clouds complain and I stand in the dark and pretend to count the notebooks. They're all I really own.

FORTY

I've been searching for a single photo for days.

There's a blank spot in the photo album for this particular photo. All of the albums are arranged in my one closet that's the size of a hall closet, because I sleep in the closet proper, so there are only two other places the photo could be.

I searched the green archival box, photo by photo, letter by letter, note by note. I searched the tin box, and threw away a dozen photos, letters, and postcards in the process. Still, no photo.

I've almost forgotten my original intent in wanting this particular photo. As I type this, I have already gone twice to two other photo albums I missed, flipped through them, and still, no photo. I wondered if I'd fooled myself. If it happened a different year than I remember. When I imagine the photo in my head, it could be from five years ago, or maybe four. There is no background to tell me who was there, which might tell me when it was, where it took place. Was it the side yard on Eastside Street, or the field area down East Bay Drive?

In any case, it's given me more time to contemplate why I want the photo in the first place, what this image of me means to me, and why that image, that specific image is what I seek at this moment.

FORTY-ONE

Three Slim Chapters of A Day: One Book, or Many, Plus Index:

       The blue carpet was one of my lovers today. I rolled around on it in a checkered pink blanket rereading *Henry & June*.

       On my desk: stack of library books. Small calendar with the most pleasing picture of a cat on the front. I think I make a face sometimes just like this cat. Two empty picture frames, pewter, scrolled edges, about the size of a slide. A few stray Kodachrome slides. A dusty audio tape with a few minutes of my mother and grandmother talking, or rather, yelling. A roll of labels with my name and address on them. A San Francisco city map. A black Sharpie. An appointment notice from the gynecologist's office. Coupons for car rentals. A little dish painted with yellow astrobrite stars, filled with quarters and a few safety pins. A stack of books I might give away. A stack of cards in plastic with words like "Enlightenment" and "Eternity" with old-time flash tattoo designs above each word. A box of colored markers. An envelope with 35mm negatives. A bill from the electric company. A clipboard smothered with papers, underneath a community college catalog, under an envelope containing an application for a writing residency. Two bookends, with twenty different-sized, different-textured notebooks. A copy of the poem "The Honey Tree" by Mary Oliver. A Crimethinc sticker. A sticker of a big black dot, courtesy of *Adbusters*. A miniature slide viewer.

                             •

What's so liberating about lying to all of your lovers? I ask my own as he lay across from me drinking green tea. He shrugged and told me that I need to be writing, that I need an audience who will notice and appreciate the sensibilities I possess underneath such questions.

FORTY-TWO

I waltz in, as much as I can waltz after a ten-hour day (working, plus 2 hour commute) (but I don't really waltz, I tramp in) and as I lift my blinds I look down at the apartment window next door. I notice the light's out.

Is it unusual that I notice the absence of a stranger? Am I considered a voyeur if I sneak peeks whenever opening or closing my blinds, or when I seat myself on the (newly-named) lustseat to have a smoke and look out at the skyline, at downtown Los Angeles? I see her on her bed, with books spilling all over, the way my apartment would be if I didn't have my bed in the walk-in closet. She has stacks of books against the wall, and sometimes magazines and notebooks all over her bed, which I once thought was a table. S. wondered aloud, "Maybe she's a grad student." I had thought, assumed, she was a writerartist.

I gulp the beer I've been craving since I stepped off the curb from the university into the street towards my bus stop. I'm holding out for the cigarette. I'm consumed with the decision: *write first? read?*

In any case, I miss the sight of her reading, working.

◆

Some notebooks stow away. The jeep may be more like a Volkswagen bus, if I can swing it, but if I can't, then it's the gray Nissan Sentra that's been stolen and come home once already. No more binders. The Canon Rebel goes side by side with a digital camera, which I will acquire in May. Dansko shoes, courtesy of K., for good restaurants. No hats, I don't look good in hats anyway, except for the cowboy hat, which is too damn hot on my head of black hair. Probably no digital voice recorder. Too much technology. The old-fashioned, hand-held tape recorder will do. The cat looks adoringly off-camera on the cover of my datebook. The black address book is sturdy and free from all those who I am no longer in touch with. Pano's has good, cheap coffee beans, I've found. My French presses are both in decent condition and looking for some travel. As it turns out, I still need the cigarettes (menthol). As it turns out, I still want the access to a bathtub, preferably clawfoot.

FORTY-THREE

Busy Signal
Wristwatch on the carpet
cups of cold coffee from early morning
phone off
the hook
the street humming
a hive
teeth on a wrist
pillow bent
a contortionist
on the floor next to the abandoned watch
timeless
fingers flexed, almost touching
the cups of cold coffee
the phone useless on the balcony
because the only voice you need
to hear
is already crying out, gasping,
sighing satiated
in your ear

•

I feel more receptive these days. Like I know what's going to happen and I want to look down, avert my gaze, and just *listen*. It may be why I have buried myself in books the way I used to as child, then a teenager. It may be why I've gone unconscious a lot in the last week, nights with a bottle of wine or the clinking of amber bottles, cool in my hand. Why I think twice before answering the phone and sometimes don't.

•

So I went to a one-day screenwriting class. At the beginning, we did the go-around where you say your name and why you're there. I had wanted to say something snarky like, "Well, I wanted to fit in with my neighborhood, Los Feliz, and thought the best way would be to write a screenplay." But we were in East L.A., and so I wasn't sure if anyone would totally get my jadedness, let alone appreciate it. Because it's often felt that way—ask anyone who has frequented Los Feliz coffeeshops—that everyone and their sister is writing a screenplay. I've dated a few of them and so have my friends. I imagine it's way more widespread than Los Feliz, but I want to only speak for what I know.

Anyway, the screenwriting class. I was fascinated. I ended up saying that I have this MFA but no experience screenwriting (I forgot about the attempts at such when I took a 16mm filmmaking class in Olympia long, long ago).

Then I sat back and watched a ray of light dance all over a stage.

In the course of five hours the ray of light spoke of the 17 seconds it takes for thoughts to become an emotion that will be transmitted to the Universe; reincarnation; the twelve archetypes we live out in this life (four of which are not chosen by us, but distributed randomly); everything as composed of vibrations; the psychic Sylvia Browne; Carl Jung; "The Forum" where one might learn what event(s), at the age of five, might have triggered the sentence we've lived under and how to combat this sentence, which can be potentially destructive; that someone is out there already writing the screenplay you want to write so you better get on it; that women fall in love with their ears while men fall in love with their eyes; and that writing from the ego is not going to produce the most passionate, heartfelt writing.

And I loved what all of these things did and did not teach me about screenwriting.

FORTY-FOUR

7:05pm: Seated at a fine restaurant in Playa del Rey. Intelligent, good-looking, interesting and sometimes flammable man sitting in front of me. I wore a thermal shirt, cut at the neck, the whole thing flashdance-esque, with a long pink and grey skirt. We are, I think, the youngest people there excluding waitstaff.

Trout with almonds. Carrot soup. Half a bottle of chardonnay. Mountain elk.

Dessert: the same one as the cover of a magazine by which we chose this restaurant.

9:15pm Began to drink a special tea by which I would break away from this particular plane for awhile. Giggled listening to Outkast blast from the flammable man's bungalow. The leaves began to breathe, the tendrils of the fig tree reached out to me.

9:45pm Readied for a walk. Observed a klieg light in the distance, decided to follow. The flammable man got ready while I made a phone call. A phone call *Out*. Then I wanted to go back *In*, immediately. It felt portentous that the flammable man's understanding of klieg light was from a Lou Reed song. I thought he might put the record on. Instead, we set out into the streets of Venice.

10:30? 11:30pm? Hard to say. The architectures of Venice surprised and delighted. Like every block was an amalgamation of architectures. I thought I saw a house with a big open porch on its second floor, and on its second floor, a large wheel, like the steering mechanism of a boat. This boat, posing as a house. It was not clear. We stood away from the house, looking, looking. We walked in the middle of the street a lot. Laughing.

Klieg light: found. In front of what we believed to be a fictitious place, of sorts. A dance party raged inside, you could see the people from the windows, and the For Lease sign was still posted.

1am The ocean. The reason I moved back to Los Angeles. To be closer to this place, the ocean I grew up near. The full moon. Jupiter, visible in the black cloth. Stood in the sand, letting my shod feet sink in, me and the flammable man sometimes looking each other full in the face during innumerable conversations, which, by the end of the whole night, seemed like a series of character sketches of people we know who are enigmas to us. Including us.

Walked almost to the Santa Monica pier. Everyone we encountered stood by, shadowed, peaceful. Hilarious uproars coming out of our mouths, and I picked up a shell. I could feel every grain of sand on my fingers and it felt comforting.

1:45am Back at the bungalow. Do I want to drink the rest of my mug of tea? No, we will have beers instead. We set up a chessboard. Conversed mostly about moves and strategies and rules, beers coaching us along.

3:30am We took pictures of each other. We are opponents on this board but the best kind: we help each other with the next move. We discuss how we want to react to the other person's move. How this is sometimes like life. I wanted to take more pictures of the flammable man but decided against it. And then: *A Love Supreme* played, on the radio, in its entirety. And then: *The Black Saint and the Sinner Lady*.

5:30am. We took to bed. Small slow breaths. Daylight threatened. Closed my eyes and fell.

FORTY-FIVE

Rejected: by an online lit journal, who told me that my writing was "fine enough" but that they don't accept material that has to do with love or sex, because other lit journals do a much better job publishing that material.

> *Uh oh*—all my writing mucks around in love and sex.
> Sometimes more often sex than love.
> It's merely a matter of me learning to channel this correctly but maybe one day all of my writing will be completely devoid of love and sex. And I will cease to exist, perhaps.

◆

Last night I reopened the loss notebook I've kept since July of 2002. The last time I had written an entry was exactly one year ago. Last night's reopening was prompted by a phone call I had while traversing my way home from work, and the conversation was cut off when I had to go underground to catch the metro home. I remembered the tears that well up in public, completely out of my control, and realized I'd have to go home and pull the notebook, contain some of the loss that was welling up, fast.

I managed to write a page but then felt compelled to read the previous entries. Halfway through reading, my forehead bloomed hot, my muscles ached, nausea roiled my guts. I took to bed.

I answered two phone calls out of the ether. I remember who called, but not what was said. I merely crawled out to say hello, then dragged myself back into the thick ether of sleep.

FORTY-SIX

1. How to not fall in love with an attentive person you meet on your travels.
2. How to walk the streets like you own them.
3. How to find a beer and a bottle opener by the light of the street lamps in downtown Guanajuato.
4. How to make chance arrangements and have your fates fall splendidly into place.
5. How to call home numerous times without an inkling of what it will cost later.
6. How to pretend like you're having fun when you're more concerned with the depression you've had and have.
7. How to find Frida Kahlo's house.
8. How to have quiet orgasms every night, alone, in a house with crucifixes on every wall.
9. How to sit quietly in a zocalo and watch people.
10. How to buy bus tickets and ignore the chanting bus schedules on the intercom.
11. How to find a hotel circled in a book with no maps.

FORTY-SEVEN

Goodbye, Willis.

Willis used to share his father's bed with me while his father, one of my best friends, slept out on the living room floor. Willis would get up next to your head and he would sneeze while you were asleep and these were not dry sneezes. Willis had an old man's meow and moved slowly unless food was for the taking. Willis had the incredibly charming habit of putting one paw on your knee as he lay next to your thigh, and he didn't mind how many beers you drank out on Capitol Hill or that you came home at 4am when the street cleaners came up Harvard Avenue. Willis seemed content in the confines of apartment 507, never trying to rush the door when it opened, like other cats might.

Willis, you will be missed.

•

From Annie Dillard's *A Writing Life*—

> *When you are stuck in a book; when you are well into writing it, and know what comes next, and yet cannot go on; when every morning for a week or a month you enter its room and turn your back on it; then the trouble is either of two things. Either the structure has forked, so the narrative, or the logic, has developed a hairline fracture that will shortly split it up the middle—or you are approaching a fatal mistake. What you had planned will not do. If you pursue your present course, the book will explode or collapse, and you do not know about it yet, quite.*

This speaks to me in many different voices (urgent whisper, unstifled shrieks, murmurs, strong, articulated tones) and I argue, tremble, nod my head, violently deny, fall asleep.

I think of the book in question. The one that is two-hundred-plus pages long, and literally sits in the corner of my single apartment, half blank of editing commentary, the other half read, line-edited, and commented on by my writing mentor at the time. It sits in the corner, like it was punished. It sometimes sits mute and sometimes I hear it mewing at me, wanting attention. Other times, it waits in the shadows of my dreams, wanting to swallow me. Sometimes, I even want to be swallowed.

◆

This is a not a musing on The Mekons, or the bay area, or drinking to excess.

This is a vignette on how it is that I dropped what I most loved, what I fell in love with in an attic, this two-hundred-plus page story that is unfinished and rough around some of its edges, dangerously jagged in some places, waiting to be smoothed and polished by my hand once again. I remember wanting to sleep next to it, to attend to it the way you do a new lover. When someone else entered the space where I wrote it, I wanted to hiss and scratch. To protect its dark blossoming. And now, its pages curl a little, and it waits. And I will return.

FORTY-EIGHT

Bend, flex. Into the fever. Let the tear drop slowly down your cheek, for it is cooling.

Sit in a hot bath even with chills. Shiver and grimace.

Try to remember the morning in order, smile wanly when you cannot.

The cost of meds the same as a week of groceries. Little white pills you wouldn't normally eat are now all that you can push down. Your voice scratches your own throat. People tell you by phone that they cannot hear you. It takes inordinate energy to lift your voice and you rather not. Your muscles ache like they want to abandon your body. You wish they could.

You think of your grandmother as you slowly switch positions on the floor. Blanket, comforter, with the fan on. Windows open. The chill. Fever spikes. Sleep, with the drone of television behind it (like when you were a kid, a baby, sick so much and television kept you company).

You've lost count of naps. They don't provide much, because you can feel the fever even through the sleep.

Later: Saltines will be allowed. Chewed in the slowest of motions. No, I mean s l o w. The overripe banana makes your nose wrinkle. Water, water.

No one is here to save you. No one is here.

It's only the fever, and you, but slowly. You are. Succumbing. To even. That.

◆

I can't physically write well after just one cigarette, and definitely not after a glass of wine or beer. But all the thoughts come in a downpour. How is it that it works that way? I suddenly want to write about every inane detail that comes by, like last night. Last night a half-bottle of white wine was gone when I sauntered away from the apartment toward a few shared bottles of

Yeti at the Indian restaurant. Lights on the patio, family of friends squished into one smallish table and one even more smallish table we pushed together. Yeti Yeti Yeti, you were good to me. A. wanted to check out the nearby strip club—I'm a strip club virgin! she cried out.   And we all know how much I love to introduce all of my friends to my local neighborhood strip joint.

Jumbo's Clown Room.

The name alone—well, you can take it from there. But anyway we walked in, got a table and it was slow. There were maybe four dancers. One who I like, and A. did too, I like her look, she said. A. sat up at the edge of the stage where I've never sat and tipped. A. gave us all dollar bills so we could all tip. I watch the dancers like I'm a strip club critic, and am probably the most benevolent critic there is. I enjoy the mirrored ceilings, the garish lights, and most of all (besides the dancers), the music. Iggy Pop, Nina Hagen, Tom Waits, Judas Priest. Very good. Very very good.

Swimming in Tecate.

I spoke to one of the dancers who offered me her stage name, making sure to tell me it was her stage name, and also told me I was born in the year of the Ox. Too true. Maybe I have an ox-y look about me. Especially being a Taurus (bull) born in the year of the Ox. I know how to dig in my heels.

After A. and her entourage left, me and S. were alone. We sat up by the stage where we've never sat together and tipped the dancer who told me her stage name. I handed her a little wad of cash personally as we walked out.

Upstairs, in my apartment, I reminded S. that I require men who challenge sexism even as they attend strip bars. He nodded. I read aloud from my notebook of two years ago. S. went to pee, and I started to cry. As I lowered my head, it began to swim. I righted myself and didn't care that S. was seeing me cry when he came out of the bathroom.

I had been telling him about how lately I'm calling my spirit back. I visualize pulling it back, often, like pulling on a long golden rope. *C'mon back now, ya hear?* I say, and gently wind the rope around my tattooed arm and pull her on back.

So in bed, I cried a little more and that was okay. It was a school night. My body was warmer and softer than it has been lately, and we decided it must definitely be all the channeled energy. I'm getting good at that. See?

FORTY-NINE

You will not love me after you read this.

The other night I was looking for the switch. Out in the desert, under a sky shot full of tiny holes, taking long luxurious swigs from a bottle of Smoking Loon chardonnay, and the switch seemed not to be there.

It is an outrage. That occasionally, it goes missing and I am left to my hedonistic and sometimes dangerous ways. Inflicting harm. Poison in the bloodstream that gets sweated out of me if I'm lucky. Dank scent of alcohol mixed in with the dirt of the desert and wood burning. The switch that tells me, sometimes, to quit drinking, let the warm feeling stay right where it is, don't compound it, is absent.

It will not please you to know that after an important, monumental, but slurred conversation with one of my camping companions about Life, and Will I Ever Want Children, and My Irrational Love For Middle Children (Never The Babies (With Some Exceptions—, Though I'm Fond Of The Oldest Children Too, But Not Like the Middle—), I stumbled off to my tent, lay down in my all-day-worn clothes, and then had to crouch low, head out the zippered door of the tent, to unleash the previously drunk wine. Bye bye Smoking Loon. Be one with the desert tonight.

Retch.

It's loving myself even in moments like these that fill me with curious (sober) wonder (but don't ask me about the next morning).

The most exciting event of the desert was not so much the incredibly loud hummingbirds with their wings that sounded like intricate purring motors, or the tiny frogs caught in T's hands, or the sky shot full of stars.

For me it was the journey there, and the stops made.

K. and I, sitting in the parking lot of Stater Bros. supermarket, Twentynine Palms Highway, after purchasing a too-large Italian club sandwich, sans the mortadella.

The checkout guy told me slyly, *I need to see your ID again*, and *You've changed your hair recently*.

I had never been to Twentynine Palms, or even a Stater Bros. before.

K. and I, pulling over on the way to the campsite, while there is still sun out, so we can drink a beer or two and talk. Her pocketknife slicing into a lime. K. and I on the tailgate of her red truck talking Annie Dillard, where we're headed, and the songs she's learning on guitar. Her guitar, and her voice, threading around my heart in the desert. Shadows on the rocks, creosote in bloom, lupine against our fingers.

All this from the bottom of my tortured heart (I wish I could draw a picture of it. It's got that line of stitches down its red pulpy mass).

FIFTY

I had the most badges in my Girl Scout troop. Troop 1610, with our faulty leaders and girls turning more and more wayward, until finally we were politely pulled from the troop. It was almost like being gently swept out of Art Group in my late twenties.

Last night, S. and I looked at the glory of my green sash, sewed and pinned badges with goofy pictures I asked him to try and decipher. He called the one with the baby carriage the Making Babies badge, the one with the cello and a ghostly red pair of hands the Grateful Dead badge, and the one with the water drop, rainbow and crystal the Lysergic Acid badge. This, from a man who was once an Eagle Scout.

We decided to pore over the Girl Scout Badge Book, which I purchased again a few years ago, when I had dreams of starting a radical grrrl scout troop, where we would learn things like how to do herbal abortions, fix car engines, and stick it to our landlords. I wanted ideas, and I also wanted a reconnection to that part of me that worked for badges, completing countless little activities that required varying levels of creativity and dedication. It probably helped that I was an only child and an overachiever.

I earned Water Wonders, Traveler, Wildlife, Tending Toddlers, Business-Wise, Math Whiz, Theater, Swimming, On My Way, Individual Sports, Sports Enthusiast, Girl Scouting Everywhere, Music Lover, and a few others. Looking at the most current offerings of badges for Juniors (the green, prickly uniforms, one level up from Brownies, and entering Cadet-hood—), I see some curious changes. My badge book is now old school, out of print. All the badges that used to have "Lover" in the title, such as Music Lover and Horse Lover have been altered to Music Fan and Horse Fan. I find that there are now offerings such as The Cooking Connection, Women's Stories, Oil Up, Looking Your Best, Jeweler, Stress Less and United We Stand.

Perhaps I'll still have to start that radical troop of my fantasies.

FIFTY-ONE

The bungalow. The sand I trail in.
The sins of before I don't count anymore.
The prayers that come in the night
in the arms of bar girls,
taxi dancers.
The sounds of freeways
or oceans I'm learning to tell
apart.
The uncomfortable shoes that look
better on the floor, decorative,
solitaire,
unmoving dancer's feet.
The blood I keep to myself.
The mirror I open myself up to
and view what I want kept secret
in the meantime.
The blanket-turned-lover.
The pillow I won't have anymore:
it wants too much room,
is a pain in the neck.
The glow of my skin when I'm alone
and when I'm out
that calls people to me:
invisible or otherwise.

•

    I have been walking back and forth on the diving board
for a long, long time. It's been months since I put on the suit and
made to dive, but it has been my whole life that I've climbed the
ladder.
    I have been pacing letting the top of my head get hot in
the sun and I have sometimes let my hair get sopping wet and

stick to the sides of my face in the rain. Walking. Back. Forth.

And it's only been recently that I've begun to look at the water. In the fall, all I could see was the water. In the winter, all I could see was the air in front of me and the long, risky plunge. Today I see the board under my feet, feel the places where my soles have weathered from the repetitive pacing, smell the ozone and the water. Today the water beckons but I cry in frustration and also because once I leave this diving board, I will be aloft. Expectant. An arrow, pointed.

Today, I see it all. Tomorrow, I dive.

FIFTY-TWO

The dive is to save myself from what I jokingly call homicide but would in fact be suicide.

Go! friends cheer, Do it! and I hear the fear and envy in their voices as they speak into work telephones or type encouragement to me on work computers.

If I don't do this the bitterness will eat me alive.

The risk is tremendous. Joblessness. Empty naked days ahead in which to write. Savings drying up into nothing but lint that could fly in the breeze of a fart.

My boss is like a wonderful mother, and when does that happen, and who turns that down?

I do.

FIFTY-THREE

"Under the Cherry Moon" by Prince flitting out from speakers into the night. A road, aptly called Lookout Mountain, and us on cold grass hearing, hearing, until we turned to each other and said, *I remember this song. I've missed it.*

And I have. It's like high school again, sitting on this cold knoll, up in the stars, view of the city, way past midnight now, clutching Bohemias and smoking cigarettes. C. bums a few from me. We partake in a ritual we made up sometime in our teens: I light the smoke, inhale. I hand her my cigarette and she lights one from mine. We switch. Each of our mouths has been on each of the cigarettes. Secret ritual, one that makes us smile, when we remember to do it. I wonder if it's the most intimate thing we share, though we ritually try to be in touch every Wednesday of every week, and it has been a good decade since we came up with that one, if not longer.

A man, standing before us, who has stood in my living room and played to the small dinner party crowd, the women seeming to tilt like flowers towards him. On this night he plays and I mostly listen, but I mostly drink my Bohemia and look at the lights far below and beyond. Later, we find chairs and station them to look out at Hollywood, our toes numb in the cool night turned early morning. On the way back to the dirt road leading us to this place, C. asks for a ride from a man in a convertible and he obliges. Three of us climb into the tiny backseat, which isn't really a backseat since we have to sit practically on the trunk, the car's so compact. I let my leg hang off the side of his white convertible. He whisks us up the winding dirt path with no railing, going good and fast for such a little road, and lets us off at the beginning of pavement. Now I really do feel like a teenager again. Only I have to drive Carrie home, and there is no one waiting up for me threatening to take my car keys away, I have to struggle for parking in my neighborhood and I have to enter my apartment alone.

It never agreed with me, the weather there. The ground never stay put. My shoes constantly at odds with the uneven earth, always leaving imprints, a way to find me; always dragging remains inside the house: flecks of mud, and if not flecks, gobs of wet dark dirt.

I returned to the desert, hidden as it is under cement and immense ribbons of black asphalt, painted with lines, dotted and whole, dotted and whole. Here, the ground doesn't stay put, but in an entirely different way: it shakes with understanding and a longing to renew. To start a new life, I returned to where I had come from. I lived alone. I created new routines that included tramping around hard crusty trails lined by ferns and dry brush, sleeping under down comforters with the windows—all of them—open, and new phone numbers like cryptic messages in my black book.

After 3, 4, 5 dates with various romantic interests, I met the one that would guarantee a plunge into icy depths, then below that, smoldering ashes, and below that, even, old, lasting fire.

The story to me, now, is old and tired, chock full of clichés I want to discard, a tree with no life, just abandoned nests and dry, whispering husks of branches.

It longs for the water that will revive it but I try not to give it any. I try to keep it starved because once is gets fed, it blossoms; it signals death to something in me that has already died. Two dozen times.

FIFTY-FOUR

1. *Fahrenheit 451* (Truffaut; not the book)
2. *Hunters of the Deep: Sharks* (documentary, battered cover)
3. lamb shank, mashed potatoes, glass of Syrah
4. touching the covers of magazines I cannot afford
5. $5 gets me *Tropic of Cancer* and *Tropic of Capricorn* in ancient paperback editions.
6. hours on my mother's couch
7. new toothbrushes (2; one for him, one for me)
8. penne pasta, salad, Cabarnet, cigarette
9. *"Bukowski: Born Into This"* at the Nuart
10. choosing pizza, Lakers game on big screen over the last day of the Diane Arbus exhibit (all a question of money...)

FIFTY-FIVE

It got into my pores.

In Las Vegas, I stopped taking showers and didn't care how crispy my curls suddenly felt. I wore the same tank top and bra for a few days and didn't care about the smoke that saturated them from the previous night's bar. I could start to see the appeal of shots drunk from test tubes, though I still managed to stick with one color instead of setting myself up for catastrophe by mixing liquors. I didn't open one book—not to read, not to write. I watched, with an absurd amount of attention, amateur strippers perform in a hamburger joint off The Strip. My body learned to move slowly in the dry heat, pacing itself in 110 degrees. I learned of Reagan's passing in an air-conditioned hotel suite, lights out, hung over, lying on top of the scratchy bedspread, which made me think of when the news of Princess Diana's death reached me—in Seattle, drunk at three in the morning, under the covers with C. in a bed belonging to neither of us, the harsh tv light making the room shift with shadows.

I'm feeling a little Las Vegas, I joked, making up a new adjective as I packed my belongings to leave the second suite in two nights. Over the span of 48 hours, I had dove into a part of myself I'd forgotten—a part that seeks destruction and chaos and wants to see some broken glass. No, actually, I fell over backwards into that part. I don't touch that place often anymore. I won't even blame it on Las Vegas. Though raw nerves dosed with gin and tonics, glossy wallet cards with photos of nude women littering the streets, painted plastic people reflecting nothing back at you while walking in casinos and Jimi Hendrix-themed slot machines might help me get to that place a touch faster.

But of course I'll go back, with new blood. Sit by the pool with different drinks, different company. Different eyes.

FIFTY-SIX

Why had I never before discovered how luxurious it feels to eat a peanut butter and jelly sandwich in the bathtub, the wind playing with the gauzy white curtain in the window above me? And why did it take so long for me to decide to listen to mariachi music on my hike up into Griffith Park, and while running in the dust downward as Nati Cano and Los Camperos burst "Tequila con Limon" y otra y otra in my ears?

As I told V., I spent an inordinate amount of time yesterday polishing and packaging up submissions (with requisite cover letters, SASEs [please pronounce it: 'sassies'] and copies) to literary journals. I am sending out my children that have as yet not been placed. Is it because one has a hole in her heart and messy hair? Is it because one likes to act out and take off her clothes inappropriately? Or is it because the third refuses to stop looking out the window at the talking crows?

It will be nice to place them someday in a nice home with steamy windows, red velvet cake baking in the oven and a cellar full of ripe apples and garlic wreaths. In a home worthy of their beautiful flaws.

This weather is reminding me of Seattle, the Seattle of overcast skies and perpetual mist. You think you feel it, but then you wonder. And then you forget about it.

That Seattle was about bars on Capitol Hill, cheap ones like Eileen's (gone now) and movie theaters and a chain Mexican restaurant on the roof of a mall that had umbrellas to protect you from the little sun and constant rain. There was the soap and scent shop, the bookstores (new, from which I could fantasize, and used, from which I bought), the game store I never set foot in but wondered of its staying power (this many people play games. We stay indoors, mostly, playing games), and the eating establishments. And the drinking ones.

Wet pavement and a constant mildew. The city moist, crying underneath the clouds. The flower shop I set foot in for once-in-awhile gifts to my favorite Seattleite, the cat who sneezed at my gifts to his human companion.

I took in about two minutes of sunlight today in Los Angeles, from the hour or two it shone. After five o'clock, the clouds came back. The gray and white blanket made me yawn. And now the music that made me think of all this just lost its course, and I am left with the last glass of red wine, the whirring of my fan (for air circulation only) and my hands, dry and not exactly yearning for pens to grasp.

[I have not even told you an inch of Seattle. I like it better that way, a snail's pace of memories.]

FIFTY-SEVEN

Franklin & Vermont

Sarah, I'm sitting near the poet, the one we always see, the one we've spied on, the one who wears black boots and has a thick skin and a poof of hair, gray, but like Richard Simmons. I heard his voice for the first time and I smelled lucidity. (Remember: I know he is a poet because S. told me—he used to see him read at open mike—at Tsunami, back when S. was the kind of person who went to open mike. We don't know that S.—). The poet is sitting nearby. The poet is carefully studying loose-leaf lined pages with writing on them. We're both grinding our pens into paper and he touches his forehead as he does this. I don't touch my forehead; I have no table. Once again, my thighs are my desk, this desk in this coffeehouse that is my office space for the night. The space AQ and I carved out tonight was ours for a while and now teems with nightlife. I have to close for now—hand hurts—but it is something that I am this much closer to him, that poet.

FIFTY-EIGHT

the budding parapsychologist is In

Amy Gerstler first rattled my bones a couple of years ago at a reading she did at Antioch. I think. My rememberance is thin. But somehow, I got hold of her work, and *Bitter Angel*, specifically, bore right through me. I remember how it tickled my blood cells. I remember memorizing its skin follicles and hair shafts. Lying in bed, touching the red cover, repeating the words over and over, whispered in a cozy bedroom in the Pacific Northwest with the rain falling outside.

AQ and I met for wine on Sunday. I feasted on fresh bread and butter imported from Normandy, AQ on charming salad with apples and walnuts and cheese. We walked not three doors down at 5 and became spectators as Amy Gerstler read from her newest book, *Ghost Girl*. It was like watching someone you have a crush on whom you've never met. Which is exactly what it is. One of my supreme writing mentors/ex-faculty mentor (he's both) was in the room, beaming, and I still didn't want to take my eyes far away from her hands holding her manuscript pages.

She told us about how she had come across the photos that are on the front and back cover of *Ghost Girl* and I thought, *this one's a Scorpio.* I asked AQ, *Do we know what sign she is?* And we did not. Gerstler told her tale, which reminded me of my own occultishness, how it springs from growing up in the library Saturdays, my obsessions with sea monsters, ghosts, and UFOs as a ten-year-old, and the fact that I began my own "X-Files" a good decade before it showed up on television (though I benefited from not being part of the FBI, this unfortunately prevented me from real research). It's the door I stopped opening awhile back, in favor of other doors, but one that's been pushed ajar again, beckoning me back. Back I go.

And: Amy Gerstler is a Scorpio.

FIFTY-NINE

bombs bursting in air

Sequestered in my near-rooftop apartment Sunday night as people used any excuse they liked to set off explosives, pieces of plastic and other parts that whistled, sizzled, screeched. Standing on the kitchen chair in the dark, I could see bursts of light play across the sky as far away, I imagine, as Koreatown. Rumbles and thuds, cracks and rat-a-tat-tats blemished the sky. No sirens, no helicopters, even. A strange, unreal night in Los Angeles.

I've wondered why it is that I've become so skittish around fireworks the last several years. I used to be the girl in the street holding sparklers, watching her mom and dad light little red sizzling things, electric flowers that scattered then putted out, and mock rockets that shot and cried out into the night. I vividly remember walking the streets of Olympia, Dec. 31, 1999. That 'Y2K' time, when we wondered what would fall and what would sustain. A group of anarchists in black roamed the streets, skipping, really, and there were fireworks shot off over top of our heads and whistles piercing from nowhere and I stepped over the detritus of low-grade explosives.

My theory is, in fact, true.

It was only a short month before that I stood in the streets of Seattle, pummeled by the sounds of the crowd around us, a nervous amoeba, tear gas floating through the air (along with other poisonous additives), my chest wracked with the foreign particles and fear—seeing people fall to the ground, collapse on the wet cement trying to breathe, trying to see, while armored tanks stood their ground and leveled more threat at us from up close. The sounds I heard that night, after a walk back up to the safer places for pho—back into downtown, the heavy CLACK CLACK CLACK, mimic of weapons, and someone blasting Jimi Hendrix's version of the Star Spangled Banner to complete the picture I found myself running into, dodging. Small crowds of people running from large booms, until someone enlightened us: It's just a sound, to scare us—there's no weapon attached to that sound! and still, it's loud enough, and there are enough people running, that we figure it's time to get out. Nothing else to do. I stood in amazement, the stretched out cords of the electric guitar coming from seemingly nowhere—a high-rise hotel? *who would lay down a soundtrack for this night, for us?*—my legs tired, my body knowing that the explosions were what was forcing me back uphill even in exhaustion, my mind stuck on the scenes of people screaming and clawing at their eyes loaded with tear gas, lungs full of something meant to drive us away.

This is where I ended, involuntarily, all fascination with street fireworks. This is where I began to sense the imminent war zone that could be created quickly, disturbingly, in familiar city streets.

SIXTY

Cast of characters: me, hair in pigtails, fresh from sleep, pink short-sleeved shirt, orange shorts and the all-important sports bra; the bespectacled man walking two Great Danes; the scruffy man coming out from a car smoking a cigarette, drinking coffee, walking a terrier; the man lying on blankets and has his camp around him in the park where camping is not permitted; Carlos, who recently began walking with a woman but who still smiles big when he sees me; the man who used to walk with a woman who once cried out to me *Beautiful!*; John, who upon seeing anyone in his path, lifts his arm to high-five, which you must do more than once—John, who tells me nearly every time I see him in his heavily accented English, You so strong! and who recently touched my tattoo and asked *Did it hurt?*; all the careful ladies dressed in casual clothes, sun visors and lipsticks; the woman wearing a metallic outfit pushing her young child in a stroller up the trail; the two men doing tai chi off-trail; the wandering woman who reads magazines as she walks with her two dogs, both of whom look like they have lived long, full lives; the bearded man walking two small black dogs that resemble bear cubs; the man who wears a baseball cap and carries hand weights, grunting at me his greeting; the men carrying walking sticks; the women younger than me, conversing up and down the route; the two men at the park's mouth who throw frisbees with the two most adorable Welsh Corgis ever, the dogs' big smiles and little waddling legs that make me want to walk up and introduce myself; the woman dressed all in white who does sun salutations; me again, coming down the trail, half-jogging, half-running, endorphins releasing, uphill, downhill, face beet-red, on my way home...

◆

This summer I decided to get moving. My partner left me to go thousands of miles south. The first night he was gone I cried and the second day I worried, chewed my nails, bought ice cream, chick patties, and a loaf of cheese and garlic bread, and I threw his blanket on the living room floor and proceeded to eat, read magazines and watch hours of comedies, bad thrillers and commercials that made me feel lonely and scared. Later that week I got angry that he left me. I didn't even want to hear his voice. Then he called to tell me there was a bomb threat where he was and I got angrier that he was putting me through this.

I also started looking at other people while ignoring the phone calls of the one I had any interest in. I contemplated freedom, bars, and heat. I went running and made my housemate my pseudo-partner. I suddenly looked forward to this aloneness. I went to meetings and lusted after someone at the meetings and went home lonely and crazed and wanting. I got courage enough to call back the man who kept calling. He wanted to go dancing.

I spent time reading and sleeping and leaving the windows open and letting lazy flies in. I went dancing and took home my dance partner and stayed up until 4am drinking and learning the body of a new lover. I lusted after the paperboy. I tried to find out where his desires led and didn't find out until later. I wrote and submitted a short story to a magazine I admire and sometimes dislike. I slept with twenty different people in my dreams and wrote letters to my partner who was still thousands of miles south. I cried and laughed and got excited over small things.

SIXTY-ONE

Cahuenga & Selma

Rereading Anne Sexton in a cool, dark coffeehouse and letting the back cover of the book peer at me, tableside. Her blue eyes, perfectly crisp dark eyebrows and her slim wrist flung back with a cigarette, so open that you almost expect the photo to speak, offer you a drink.

She was silenced by her own hand.

My stomach growls. A new set of folks come into the place. I have the best seat in the house, the iced coffee is pitch perfect. I listen contentedly as the woman nearby, who had a table to herself, packs up her big earphones like ear muffs, her laptop, various plastic bags, books, and zips various pouches and messenger bags ups and leaves. All of her noises are pleasing to me, much in the way that listening to someone spritz cleaning fluid on a table is pleasing to me. Almost unexplainable.

I feel built for this leather chair and its ottoman. I'm a fixture in this portable living room, in a part of Hollywood I don't pay rent on.

All of this re-reading, during Mercury retrograde, seems fitting. The hammering of details. Attention, attention.

Rereading the death notebooks reminds me that a year ago at this time I was thoroughly entrenched in a death trance of my own, tiptoeing the murk, stirring the sediment of the swampy bottoms and wandering past the bottomfeeders.

I am finally understanding the nuance of Sharon Olds's broken lines, and the characters that come stumbling, dancing, flying out of Amy Gerstler's fingers...

◆

It is a strange day when I find myself on the verge of leaving the safe haven of friends and foggy mornings six hundred miles north of my abode, when an email intercepts my thoughts on leaving and arriving to tell me, in Spanish, that if I want to see this little girl again I have to pay $5 and a pair of red underwear. Attached is a scanned photo of me, naked in a playpen, age one, summer on my skin and mouth open in glee, little teeth bared. This, from the man who wanted to finger my rosebud earrings twelve years ago, in a bungalow classroom on a Wednesday night, in a class called The Anthropology of Religion, Magic and Witchcraft, and who did sundry other things to me that made me yelp and sweat and glimmer. Because the photo shows me tabla rasa and blissful, and because he threw away all the later collected panties, including their glass enclosure, I think: *You can keep the picture.*

SIXTY-TWO

Simple rules of August
1. Try to refrain from re-reading Sylvia Plath's journals.
2. Awake from the Taurean lap of naps and luxury to hike in the sun up the trail you fondly call your own.
3. Smell the air. Remember what August does to you. Remember what September, October usually mean.

SIXTY-THREE

(1)
Monday-Wednesday: I was reading a library copy of *The Myth of Solid Ground: Earthquakes, Prediction, and the Fault Line Between Reason and Faith* by David L. Ulin.

(2)
Thursday: I visited K. in Portland and she gave me a brand-new copy of a book.

(3)
Thursday: We began hearing reports of Mt. St. Helens and the rumbles under its surface.

(4)
Friday: On the way from Olympia to Centralia, Washington, I pointed out to P. the bizarre arrow-like clouds, three of them, which seemed to point at Mt. St. Helens.

(5)
Sunday: I came home to California and embarked on a little paper-mining expedition in my apartment. I came across these notes, written August 22, 1993:

House of Earthquakes

She imbibes the rich orange liquid stationed at her side. She swallows it every weekend without fail and follows her aching daughter around, haunting, bellowing, dancing evil dances. The orange fluid lubricates her insides and allows the earthquakes visibility. She thrashes on the couch and in her faulty steps. The tremors rock her pores, her bloated body, face, and splash out along her already saturated brain, rippling off into her recesses. Her daughter watches often with the calmness of a sphinx and occasionally responds with a tumult of her own, dry earthquakes and thunder, lightning flash of brass figurines that thud on carpeted floors. She closes the door until the signs say the temblors are lessening. All week the mother trembles, huddles from nervousness, hides her twitches. But the earthquakes return and every bottle in its place under the sink rattles until they are empty, then fallen, until they finally transform into harmless, silent glass.

When her daughter leaves on Friday, she knows she will return to earthquake country. Before, the quakes had been as reasonable as quakes can be, with much time in between, and helpful telltale rumblings. Leaning against her mother now, she would easily fall into gaping crevices, fall into open and uncertain air. Later, she wonders how her mother will survive when no one is there to watch, monitor, react.

SIXTY-FOUR

Expensive ghosts:

     In the midst of purging, dumping loads of sometimes decades-old negatives and random shots of blurred heads, I found two rolls of black and white film that needed developing. I no longer remember the darkroom. I took the film in to the local drugstore and waited.

     Almost thirty dollars later—thirty dollars I really should not be spending on mysteries—I have the photographs. One roll is a series of shots from a Butoh performance given at an all day fair at the college I graduated from. In the photos, men and women clad in white togas, completely covered in white make-up, contort their faces and bodies, and some move what looks to be a large white egg around the perimeter of their space or their bodies. One photo captures the "audience"—a nuclear family sitting on a grassy knoll, very much surprised to see a ghoulish figure painstakingly manipulating this large white egg near them. One photo features a woman I am still acquainted with, who I in fact went camping with in Joshua Tree earlier this year, and who is now pregnant. The photos have an unfocused quality though they are in focus.

     The next roll of film features us, the us behind the camera, the same day or series of days around the fair. There is Sarah and B. cooking in our kitchen. There is Sarah and D., posed, smiling. There is me sitting on P.'s lap. These were the days when my hair was long and I hadn't asked Sarah to cut some bangs for me yet. I could wear the 1960s brown tropical bikini top because it still fit and it was early summer in Olympia. There is me, saluting the photographer with a plastic cup of beer. And in between, there are random photographs of a television set (on), the front page of a newspaper, the local movie theaters, the apartment I lived in, an apartment whose inhabitants are strangers to me, and views that are not the same anymore. And that's just it: these photographs could be called, as a collection, "The Views That Are Not the Same Anymore." But still, I wish I had not paid nearly thirty dollars for these Views...

SIXTY-FIVE

Landed in San Luis Obispo after an adrenaline-awash day of driving Highway 1 with Arabic lilts camouflaging the car from cliff's edge. Cambria (by the Sea) was full of jokes made of wood and sugar and all I wanted was hot coffee and to throw my black bag somewhere it could land. We found that somewhere, thankfully, before the fog got worse and the sun buried itself. A desultory tour of possibilities: the one that proved best was the one with pool and spa, open late, lit for evening plunges. After a dinner in a conformed dorm room downtown and a drive through streets placed around a university (known for what?), we changed into appropriate attire for baptism or beaches and braved the bone-chilling wind and black night suffused with fog. We became one with the water, us. The bubbles of our cauldron seared our skins and with glee we played and splashed, sea horses in hell, mist clinging to our top halves that were stuck out in the unforgiving air. For a time we shared the bubbly puddle with a man and his baby son who entertained themselves, and there was nothing for us to do but watch, sitting in this perfect circle as we were. When you made for the bigger pond, icy rectangle, I heard myself shriek: the shriek came from a place inside me where I hide the unwrapped lollipops stuck with bits of hair and lint; the pages torn out of magazines with humans glossy-faced, luring; the secret desires of watching others' behaviors you know will not go unpunished. You threw yourself in the cold pocket of wet, I shrieked, and when your seal head emerged and I saw your dark hair slicked back, teeth bared, I began loving you in a new way— your essence of fire undoused by even this eight feet of water you tread. And from that night on, I knew that this type of love was born there and we would never go back to interrogate or assess it. San Luis Obispo. That was it.

SIXTY-SIX

As beautiful as the palm trees are, as placid as the sky looks, I am still disturbed at the world I find myself in.

It is not just this election and the aftermath I can only guess at that has me thirsty for inspiration; in the last several weeks I have found myself only wanting to see films that might leave an impression on me that widens the little periscopes I usually look through—see films, read stories, that might remind me that for every anti-choice essay paper I grade, there are a thousand viewpoints that are in dissonance to that—see films, read stories, hear words that remind me that for every girl I teach who does not have the freedom to walk off the detention center grounds, there are countless pearls of wisdom forming inside that very girl—reminders that the 'radicals' I associated with are even more radical now just by virtue of the election (and this makes my heart race)—reminders that I've always preferred open-ended questions over answers, and this is one of those perfect moments...

"Are there two ways of knowing the world—a submissive and a devouring way? They end up roughly the same place." Anne Carson, from *Plainwater*.

Autumn. Fall. The verb 'to fall.' I sit hot and stewing all summer, cauldron of plans. In August I start anew and by September, the first plans are locked into place. A dry leaf crackles under my shoes. I shiver. It's time to half-close the windows that have been open since March. The night comes faster, racing with its beacon of black light. I rumble and stir when the days shorten, mourn the loss of summer—for a minute—and then join hands once again with Pluto and it's time to delve deep into where I never want to go the rest of the year. The veins in the dark red leaves remind me of my feelings, locked to the outside of my body where other people can see. Some will touch. I wince at this attention, sometimes hide deeper in the trees. When I stop trying to prevent endless summer it is easier to fall. And we are halfway to spring with its particular box of pink petals, hormones and promise of new fruits and bedmates.

Autumn is my molting. It's conceivably the point at which I do or undo. It contains the unraveling. The scarves I intended to protect my neck for winter come undone and it is time to pick up the needles once again, reknit, re-construct, with an eye only on the work, my fingers, these hands, the connection between these eyes and fingers and all the lifeblood in between, the synapses snapping like the crunchy dead leaves under the shoes that ceremoniously cloak my feet—hiding the roots that jump and tendril down to the deep.

SIXTY-SEVEN

Oakland

The drive up into the cemetery, with the windows going up and down, a nod to the changing temperatures: the sun, the clouds, interruption of fog.

The headstones that catch my eye: Benjamin Saltman's. *Severance, Risk, Lux.*

The music: a woman growling *you're evil, you're evil* and the sun peeking out again, giving us a delicious wink. Up the curving drive sideswiping walkers and a jogger who sidles by, scaring Sarah, our driver on this excursion.

We are in a black car.

We come upon mausoleums. Surnames engraved on the face of tall stone constructions. We see the buried family Lux. The music turns into that classical piece, the one reminiscent of chaos and sounds as if angels are contemplating their falls from grace and Sarah flicks the radio off hurriedly.

We laugh a little hysterically.

I run out to look at the inside of a mausoleum and inside, I see years of dust, three stems of discarded fake pink roses, and the crypts that look like drawers with names on them, and one that has a name and no date etched on it. A lone wheelbarrow. Gardening tools. I run back. One of the mausoleums has doors held closed by a chain. The others' ornate doors are like bars, a prison. We see the backs of houses that face all this hill and stone. Driving through the rest of the grounds, we spot an Ortiz, a Bullerdyck.

Chapel of the Chimes, columbarium and crematorium. "Before Need." The various incarnations of the bible displayed in glass cases. Light comes down from skylights, the light mixes with the smell of loamy soil, the humidity thick as plants carelessly grow. Ornate lettering.

Each room opening into another, every room lined with the dead.

The trickle of water fountains, a room filled with live birds and the ever-present tiles. The gold tones, lack of darkness. Scripture above doorways. Seven sacred poems in a case, opened to one about sorrows. Stones engraved. The work of the engraver: templates? stencils?

John Lee Hooker, here we are the day before your birthday, and here you lie.

The outside world again. The reassuring sun filtering into an early fall and the fog seeping in at the corners.

SIXTY-EIGHT

Pasadena

No one wanted to go see this movie with me. I could not understand why. The previews we'd seen showed images of dark chasms, ice, and hinted at something very difficult and disturbing that happened between two friends. I was enchanted from the start.

I ended up alone on a Saturday in Pasadena, a place I never go, to see *Touching the Void* on a warmish afternoon in February. There were about ten people in the audience.

What I saw was a filmic metaphor that stretched for the movie's entirety. While I could be lulled by the landscapes I could also be awestruck by them, wondering at the force of the winds, the snow, the danger created between the landscape and harsh climate. That two people wanted to climb an ominous mountain face was almost not even part of the story I experienced; I was more taken with the stories underneath—the story of cutting the rope, the story of knowing your own death has every possibility of happening in the matter of hours, the story of where your mind will go when you are on the verge of collapsing in on yourself, the story of true, deep forgiveness, but mostly this: the story of deciding, finally, that if you cannot go up, then you must go down, deeper, into the dark, into the place you have always been coached, scolded and warned to avoid. For many it's that place you imagine you will go to and never return from, a place of suffering and the end. And it is there, that place, that you find your way out.

Piece by piece my belongings are moving further into the city. My view will change from seeing the lights of downtown from afar to seeing the tall buildings, much closer, on Wilshire Boulevard. I will be walking distance from the HMS Bounty, which excites and scares me (picturing myself walking there for a whiskey...daily...). I am seven days from saying goodbye to the place I have known intimately for three years: the first place I have lived truly alone and the first place I have lived since returning from afar to settle back into Los Angeles after an eight year absence.

Now, a new adventure.

SIXTY-NINE

This last ten days, no—two weeks—has been full of misadventure, misfortune and woe, with occasional outbursts of song. I feel I have been made to learn things fast, faster than I'd ever want, and since life is as it is, I have been made to learn things I didn't even set out to get an education in. Alright. Let me try and pass the test.

Two cats with opposite temperaments and minor maladies that have me puzzled, sleepless. A book I cannot seem to get back into but I try, I try. The nuances of living in a new apartment, a new neighborhood, and even worse parking than before. Sleeping in a new bed. Feeling closer to the helicopters. *Hey, champurrado!* being yelled twice a day in a deep and beautiful voice up and down my (new) street. Reminding my grandmother of who I am. Looking into the eyes of my mother and wanting to cry, looking away. A squat, two-foot Douglas fir ringed with lights and a mermaid under its branches, my first holiday tree in years. No elevators. Vomiting. Sobbing while driving. Trying to herd numerous juvenile offenders of different stripes into writing. A significant Sunday night. Sally Timms and her melody following me through the streets: *I'm just a junkyard barge off the coast of New Jersey and I don't know where I'm going to...* Neko Case making me cry in the balcony of the El Rey. The pain that shoots from my heart through my left arm into my shoulder and around my back. The key not fitting in the door.

•

My palm lived through it all—my palm lives today, still, older, perhaps tighter and with more lines, lines from holding pencils taut in my left hand then graduating to pens, lines from grasping utensils and also scooping up rum-laden fruits from a bowl in the middle of South Dakota, lines that tell stories of fists clenched and pillows struck and glass, held then flung; my palm patiently waited for the grasp of the most compatible hand, while grabbing and letting go of the most physically attractive, the sexiest, the most dangerous of other palms; connected to my arm, my palm, composed of rough skin that is not as brown as the parts of my skin that see sunlight; my palm has worked at schools, retail stores, handed anti-perspirant to young women and pushed the shopping carts of old women; my palm, one of a twin, held the hands of all children not of me; lovers licked and kissed the tender underside of my hand; palm outstretched, it guided free things to my mouth, candy, drugs, food; my palm exists as one of my appendages, the one that experiences the heat, the roughness, the cool and the ice of the world; my palm, this one that grasps a pen at yet another bus stop...

◆

I was Catalina, Oxford, Serrano. I was Western. I was a joint passed on 3rd. I was greetings shouted across the street. I was prepaid cellular. I was white shoeprints on wet asphalt. I was gutter runoff. I was sitting on the curb smoking a pipe. I was España I was discounted audio and I was hot sauna. I was Council Street. I was long lines at post office. I was green nylon pants. I was muddy paths. I was orange cones and clutched umbrella. I was dark clouds coming.   I was plastic bottle being emptied of water. I was toothy grin in wrinkled face. I was locked library doors and I was mountains in the distance. I was a memory slipping away. I was hip hop from an upstairs window and I was stop sign and I was dirty dogs tied to the pole. I was gold dog and I was wet blue rug. I was El Sereno and I was home.

You were too.

SEVENTY

A nap at 9:30pm, an altogether unusual time for a nap. The black and white cat under my arm, my hand resting on her white bib. I awoke to feeling seared. Something scared her and she awoke, scratching, and the cat in me wondered if she had done it purposely. She's a queen that way, alright. She walks like a bear and our boyfriend—oh, excuse me—*my* boyfriend compares us constantly. Fumbling for alcohol pads in the dark, the gentle blotting of blood in my palm, a place I have never had pierced just this way. Springlet of red. Quiet dark of night as I rise again to read, immersed in poetry all evening, even during the nap while the heater whirred, forgetting what the meteorologist termed "parade of storms" on the maps, the place where he meant I was, we were. The foggy greys swirled, a most unbecoming parade. I do dislike the self-awareness of parades; always preferred the anarchist kind. Still true. Glad to have watched the parade of storms pass, the beads of water they flung still clinging to the earth.

◆

Lime-scented candle. If hot had a smell, this would be it. Gentle lapping of cat's tongue on small pool of water. Candle flickers. Dirty flecks in the wine that are not old cork. The syrupy cheap. The calico mottling. The goose and gosling. Frenetic in stereo. Staving off Sylvia Plath, as though her writing is a virus I catch, come down with. I cannot be held responsible for what happens next. She is a fever to me. I want to point my finger and have thunderbolts fire. I know they're there, lodged deep in my knuckles. There must be a good reason I'm left-handed.

Queenly white breast puffed out on this cat, fur soft as feathers.

I'm not sure what the meaning of the spider in our sink is, or why December 21, 2012 has suddenly flung itself up over and over in my hapless imagination. It will be the fortieth birthday, I think, of someone I know, someone I thought I was in love with for a pinpoint, no, a pinwheel of time. I walk from room to room and the candle laughs a fuck you at me, throwing its scent around, casting memories like shadows. I'm not sure what will happen when the flame burns down the wick, the pool of wax acquiesces, the tangy lime flower explodes in the air.

SEVENTY-ONE

Santa Monica

In winter it's commonplace to scoot the old cracked windows up, the height of a sitting cat. It is for this that I moved one thousand miles south. I was no longer content with something called summer that lasted a pittance. Like a nickel thrown into a thirsty woman's cup. *Clang.*

What better place to inaugurate that moment than the ocean, in winter, alone, sunset just having passed, and still warm enough from the walk to not need a sweater.

Gaps between lines. Squares. Intersections. I am at Montana and Ocean. The ocean and Montana will never meet, but they do here.

Who wouldn't love to walk daily with views like this. In my neighborhoods you must bypass gum, gunk, dog shit, trash, sewer smells and more. Of course, it is alive in a different way.

There is almost a pain about coming here. Because the ocean, close to it, is where I have always wanted to live. Always.

The Ferris Wheel. I'm looking at it from the opposite direction than the last time I saw it, when I was with him. Passing the bungalows and the blond men casually walking down Montana, I yearn for something specific, but mostly for what might have been.

I get an invitation to do some facilitation work for an anti-oppression training and I am reminded that this is just one of my skills.

I am reminded that in a not so recent past, I attended workshops as often as possible, actively learning and unlearning things that ended in -ism, and I danced, and I acted, and I wrote and I studied. I went to Portland and to Seattle to get my fix of trainings and modules and lessons. I wrote articles, debated fine points. I rode my bicycle up and over the hill and back again with a fleet of like-minded. I held the video camera and shot the rolls of film. I marched and paraded and edited down reels. Booked my weeks far in advance. Pressed play. Learned to yell for my life. Painted and posed naked. Deposited checks. Copied handouts. Upped the volume. Held the forum. Shouted into megaphone. Spoke into the microphone. Locked arms. Pasted up. Talked finance. Created the zines. Recruited. Presented, established, cooperated. Cooked down herbal decoctions. Counseled women whose shoes I'd been in. Listened. Listened. Floated. Floated. Wore the protective mask. Sold the tickets, raised the money. Handed the books out. Turned out the lights at the end of the night.

◆

I do believe that Hunter S. Thompson is my first, personal literary icon to die in my lifetime.

I could think of a few others—Gloria Anzaldúa, Susan Sontag—but this one, strangely, plunges deeper. I say 'strangely' because it is strange. I read *Hell's Angels* when I was fifteen. Over the years I read his books of correspondence, watched the films based on his life, decided that if I ever have a daughter, she will have Hunter somewhere in her name. At sixteen, I moved on to *Fear and Loathing in Las Vegas* and reading this while in Catholic school in Los Angeles was more than a little mind-blowing. I was already experimenting with drugs, but reading this book, at that age, at that moment in my life, crystallized a thought to me—one that I still find strange, and can only speak about astrologically, now (for those with interest: my natal chart has Neptune in the 12th house—and that's just the tip of the iceberg)—where was my female Hunter S. Thompson figure? Where could I find her, and if I couldn't find her, how in this lifetime could I become her? Not a genius thought from a sixteen-year-old mind: just strange. Perhaps stranger when still crystallized—having imploded, exploded, reformed—in the mind of a thirty-one-year-old.

Then, perhaps, not.

SEVENTY-TWO

Rain the last five days.

This pocket of hope that says, When the rain stops, it will be over. Only to face sheets of water and nuggets of hail being flung from the sky minutes, hours later.

[The saying that insanity is doing the same thing over and over again and expecting a different result.]

I keep feeling, like, this is IT. Or when the rain gets louder, so loud you have to raise your voice, so loud I think, it cannot get any louder, it does. The wetness sticking to the lungs. The lulls that feels anything but peaceful. Looking out the kitchen window of the third floor apartment, I spy on the clouds. The Equitable Building is the tallest on the horizon, the building that S. says reminds him of a tombstone, grave marker in the sky. [Think of it: EQUITABLE etched on a stone in a cemetery.] I watch the building and take note of where the clouds hover around it. I squeeze liquid soap on a sponge, run cold water (the basement is flooded; water is pumping out, running down the stone steps to the sidewalks and the pilot cannot be lit), soap up last night's dishes, and I watch the Equitable Building framed by blue then by light gray and white then by dark gray. Borders and frames in the rectangle of my window. If I stand further left, out the same window I will see the dark gray clouds like a mountain range coming from the direction of the ocean.

I've seen more thunder and lightning in the last five days than I have ever seen in my whole life.

Saturday we went out into the flooded streets for free live music in a bar. Inside, dark, red, brown, it was as if there was no rain. [Rain/no rain.]

Inside the warm movie theater on Sunday, getting lost in the film, the depictions of sweat and work and dedication all fell away when we stepped into the lobby and could see the downpour from the glass doors.

[What else can you do but step into the new liquor store, inhale the smell of paint that's not rain and asphalt, not rain and dog hair, not rain and grass clods? There is nothing else to do but buy a 12 pack, go home, make dinner. The furnace won't light, so bring out the extra blankets. Watch more movies from a perch on the loveseat. Finger the fringe of the wool blanket.]

Missed excursions: my mother's house, a horror film, the library, the grocery store, the dance club, the gym, the poetry reading, the classroom, the job. [The rain is soaking my checkbook and my cheap shoes.]

Perhaps the only upside is the thunder and lightning. [The roar of the sky makes me giddy.]

Forced indoors, I have emptied two moving boxes of their contents and rearranged the contents throughout the apartment and into another, smaller box; helped put posters up on the white walls; eaten various delicious meals prepared not by me and from expensive cookbooks; wandered the worldwide web like a drunk flaneur; [listened to the water drip, crash, spill, pitter-patter]; sighed too often; skimmed a stack of library books I'd previously forgotten; rearranged papers, recycled, created new clipboards fat with papers, and composed new lists. [And still, the storm feels like it's won.]

SEVENTY-THREE

AQ put it best when she said that perhaps what was lacking here in Los Angeles was the sense of play around something like the Academy Awards. In this industry-heavy place, it would be hard to have a sense of humor about the whole event and the events around the event when so many people we know or friends of people we know are so heavily invested in The Industry.

The last time I watched the Oscars with any sort of attention span was at Sarah and Andy's place on Edgemont, complete with 1000 pieces of food and many bottles of wine and live entertainment during commercials provided by Chris Sand, the Sandman. There was still room to discuss the awards show as it unfolded, laugh our asses off, or just ignore it in favor of good conversation. Susan knitted, I lounged on the floor, Sandman played, our hosts entertained.

In Olympia the Oscars show was an event. Each year the Capitol Theater hosted an Oscars bash, just as they are this year. We dressed up, walked down to the theater in our vintage gowns and patchwork suits. I clutched a little wad of cash for champagne. P. and I found seats in the balcony and soon, various friends and acquaintances would show up and find their seats throughout the theater. Many champagne glasses later (purchased in the mezzanine, where there were television screens broadcasting the show so one would not have to miss anything while waiting in line) our legs might be splayed on the seat in front of us (it is this kind of theater, the best kind), and we'd be hootin' and hollerin' at the screen, calling out hello to a friend we saw sashaying down the aisle on the ground floor, chuckling at someone's well-placed comments on whomever was crossing the stage on this big wide screen, broadcast live from Los Angeles. We had live hosts for the in-between and prizes were given away if you had the winning ticket stub. P. drunkenly ran down the curving stairway amidst the crowds and jumped into Leon's arms; I laughed until I cried.

Olympia, the place I spent eight years incubating in before I would return home. I miss those nights in Olympia, strolling home in the cold, my little wad of cash spent, my arm in P.'s, teetering in the heels I wore perhaps two nights a year, wondering about the fortune teller who told me when I was thirteen that I would win the highest award in my field when I was all grown up. At thirteen I envisioned the Oscars, a clip from the film I created playing behind me, the heavy icon in my hands congratulating me for excellence in cinematography.

SEVENTY-FOUR

(March 2005)
New to me this year + various accomplishments and other sundry things:
quitting smoking (the one cigarette a day I've had for the last several years)
Koreatown (living in)
a man who is almost 40 (the one I live with)
Law & Order SVU
Sandy, Kathy, Tess
exercising a minimum of four days per week
getting stuck with needles
weddings of long-time close friends
being on the inside of something I was once on the outside of
The Office (original) on dvd
paying less than $375 a month to live in Los Angeles
pregnant friends
Don DeLillo
Ms. Martha Kinney and *Heartless Horse*
learning more about AQ, happily
coordinating a literary reading series (with AQ, who I learn more about, happily)
getting bent
fumbling with the shut-off switch of alcohol intake
a return to steam rooms and saunas
teaching creative writing to boys
Cali(coco) and Lupita(pie)
the merits of the two-day work week
Ecuador (August-September '05)
letting go (as always)

•

~~I have been dreaming a lot lately.~~

I always dream a lot. I'm remembering the dreams, but most importantly, remembering to type them up. I repeat certain elements to myself all day if I have to, in order to retain their essence to be able to write them down later. Tofu, cockroaches, weddings, pregnant. *Tofu, cockroaches, weddings, pregnant.*

Open the cellar door; receive.

My mind as of late is being taken up with things like the essay I plan to write about Vincent D'Onofrio; what happens when you rubberband written messages to glasses of water and then drink them; how to find very particular Bugs Bunny cartoons that I need to re-view (esp. one featuring Porky Pig, in which he is in a boat, falls asleep, then has underwater adventures/nightmares); artificial insemination; the essay I plan to write about why I like to throw back handfuls of pills into my mouth and how I one time swallowed a pair of earrings by accident this way; contemplating the purchase of a bed frame: the first biggest purchase made in conjunction with my sweetheart; reuniting with my long lost gray Formica table, that now moonlights as my desk, where all things happen; what to write next; how to whittle down the stack of library books without feeling I am depriving myself. Oh, and what I might do for a paying job come April 15.

◆

Last Friday was my first poetry workshop in a long, long time. We were armed with at least three pages of poetry each, one bottle of wine per head, homemade pasta salad with crunchy, sweet vegetables, chips, salsa and bean dip.

T. didn't just have the lights low: her electricity was down to just a couple sockets working throughout the apartment. Candles everywhere, and all the Catholic iconography standing out more richly, bolder than their usual bold. I moored into my little comfy space on the hardwood floor in front of the closed and painted over fireplace, where I sit one Friday per month and talk writing with T. and AQ, talk that twists and turns, and I'm reminded of how much I miss this particular type of exchange. Our salon of sorts. Last time we covered such subjects as the children's show *Davey & Goliath* with T. doing a remarkable imitation of Goliath and recounting an episode she saw recently. Last time, or the time before, it was pouring rain and the lights kept dimming in time with the thunder and lightning, while we spoke of astrology, spell-casting. Last time, a strange tap tap tap sounded out of nowhere and AQ invited it in in her welcoming way. I'm reminded, too, that it's not just this kind of exchange I miss, but this kind of Exchange, where I can wander down a dark hallway and laugh at the sudden slap of the blinds in the candle-lit bathroom window, murmur at the fast surprise dim of a light bulb.

But this was a poetry workshop, and there was Shiraz, and Syrah and Merlot, and a pile of poetry journals before us, and comments written on paper and elucidated in air. I got help with line breaks. I tried to articulate the rhythm of the poetry I was reading into something like a chantey. I've missed the invisible cursive we can write in the air as friends who are working on writing together, in a living room, with no time constraint on the night. Indeed, AQ and I can never seem to leave before one a.m. And we've upped the ante to two Fridays a month.

SEVENTY-FIVE

Vermont & Beverly

Okay, stop whining about your 'minor headache.' That you can even call it minor is a positive thing. You are in the studio of an internet (ahem) radio station and there is plenty to look at all over the walls, and there is even that certain smell you like, that light mildewed carpet scent that reminds you of band practice in the garage and the boys you loved whose attention you wanted, and the loveability of people who don't give a shit that the place is a mess. If you could peel back the first layer of band flyers, record albums, various political posters, newspaper clippings and photos of someone's arm or half of their face, what would be left? A quivering wall of flesh? No, that is so vaginal-sounding. Your headache is lessening, becoming minor minor. Not even a constellation, not an Ursa Minor, less than, so much less than. The dj is playing 80s music and you feel that twitch in your eye muscles, wonder if the blue underneath your eyes still looks blue, bruised, and does your father really look Aztec like your boyfriend said, and if this 80s music thread is going to last and how Hunter S. Thompson would have written this scene.

You are thinking of people to get to know better. The dj is playing old David Bowie. He is quietly trying to pierce your heart with what he loves, knowing or not knowing that it is what you love, too.

You flash on your friend the monk. How his birthday just passed and you thought of him all day but did not email him, did not send a card in advance. You feel he is somehow beyond birthdays now (it makes you want to cry) and he is beyond all the plans you are making, the ones you vowed never to make, like living with a lover again, and taking on two new cats, and getting married—the monk is in a West Virginia monastery and he is him. You are you. Many miles separate and it makes you want to cry. You once thought you would marry each other for the potential gift registry at Dees in tiny downtown Olympia.

You just fucking spilled beer all across his Husker Dü album! He wasn't looking. You wipe it down with a dirty canvas bag that isn't yours on the table that isn't yours. You think for the third time tonight how much your innermost soul would like some Purell in here. You touched the community bottle opener one too many times.

Baby doll high up in a corner with pink and white checked dress silkscreened with the name of the station. Plastic cup with plastic spoon and knife. A very slight smell of reefer. A man with thready limbs, knobby veins, leaning over a turntable.

It wasn't even Bowie earlier, You. It was a wanna-be. Now you are listening to Bowie. This man before you knows how to enter music. You used to remember how and do it more often.

You wonder why you must always succumb. Especially in italics. Like that. *Succumb*.

A newspaper clipping: "Girl Scouts Burn U.S. Flags—Out of Respect for Old Glory."

Your fingers are sticky. And dry.

A poster: "WE ARE A WEBCAST STATION." Underneath that, in red marker, "Gorilla." A homemade cardboard sign, blue, with red marker letters: "be your values." A small, dorm refrigerator, covered in stickers. "Our phone number: xxx-xxxx" on a tattered, hole-punched paper, taped to a wooden shelf. A smurf figurine playing guitar.

You wish you could fuck him in here. He is playing Devo. That's why you want to fuck him and also because of his thready limbs and knobby veins and his short, short hair and his shiny black shoes.

A poster for a vintage film called "Cobra Woman." A blue photocopied poster of someone in their plaid underpants, and you can't tell if it's their front or back end. And that wasn't even Devo anyway, it was Gary Neuman!

You look out the window and watch someone jog/shuffle across Beverly. You realize: This is your neighborhood, baby! Get used to it!

SEVENTY-SIX

Dolores and Robert, circa late 1960s, Pomona Fair photo booth
Virgo, Gemini
vodka, whiskey
high heels, black rubber soles
Lola, Roberto
manicures, finger bandages
East Los, San Joaquin Valley
station wagon, El Camino
Dee, Bob
romance and horror, true crime
September 11, Memorial Day
gossip columns, daily paper
blue veins, tattoos

•

::finish writing the story I began after a nap, an hour before my birthday party, with the abducted girl as narrator
::think: *astrological ethnography.*
::stay up later and later.
::keep drinking yerba mate and green teas daily.
::imagine the finish line of June
::get everything you wanted out of the Jenny Holzer and Cindy Sherman books; you can't afford to buy them, so please, return them to the library so someone else can take a look at them.
::keep reading Robert Lowell, Elizabeth Bishop, and forget that you were never properly taught these poets.
::mend the dress and wash the cats
::keep taking deep breaths
::borrow gardening books and envision your mother's backyard and what you will do with it someday
::write your religious upbringing, start to finish. Marvel at how unfinished it will be.

::work on the anthology with T. and AQ
::think deeply about the show *Carnivale*. Daydream and write what you would say if you were to join them on the road. Or what you would do in Brother Justin's church.
::make blueberry and pineapple shakes
::book the flight to Ecuador
::create a 10 day party in your hotel room this month
::be not afraid to sing

◆

I like the sound of this paper crackling.

She felt her insides to be tunnels of black blue shadows and her blood providing the only light.

The gates and fences. The divisions between preschool and kindergarten.

I didn't like my mother much as a kid.

When I said I was dying from the heat in here, he finally seemed to break out of his stupor and hear me.

Children have been playing outside my window, down below, for a good hour.

One of my powers I don't talk about is my ability to see prey.

SEVENTY-SEVEN

Like runny eggs. Por supuesto, por supuesto. Walking in the woods without a light. That's the bad thing about watching an entire season of *The Sopranos* in two nights. Firecracker evening sky. Beads, small silver hands and hummingbirds. Tart little tomatoes. Leg hanging off the bed with all of those slasher images in your head. Swept up in the sangria waterfall. Love lov luv all over until it oozes you to sleep. Hammock sleep, the best kind of sleep. Dirt road and green valley meet. New sandals and necklace. When you met your life again under the hands of a gray-bearded man and you were well, you were well and it opened you, it opened you until you were talking in chants. You always talk to yourself. You were caught today on 1st Street. And we will start our dreams from scratch from a table in Albuquerque, New Mexico. And we will start our dreams from this deck underneath stars. And we will start our dreams from this pinprick in the sky, or that. And we will forgive and forget our nightmares. They only want some attention. Like the black and white cat under our palms. Like the sirens cleaving traffic. Like the smallest hummingbird searching for her sugar water.

◆

     I need to purchase some pink tablets, a money belt, and a cheap pair of flip-flops. Going through the closet for the right shoes to wear at the wedding. Handing out house keys. Listening to the drip of the new showerhead, installed by the Department of Water & Power not two months earlier. Phone orders of chicken vindaloo and saag paneer. Burrowing in blankets past the alarm. Dreaming of running mightily for hours. Contemplating the darker of the stories. Touching artist books and admiring their bindings. Envisioning three weeks of nothing I must do, except for said wedding and related events. Farewell to cats, who will be left in good company. I will be in a city that is said to have more internet cafes than any other in the world, so I may check in from time to time. So close to the equator and so high up (9200 feet), I wonder what my dreams will bring. Will it be like a cat leaving dead birds at my door? Will it be like opening the wardrobe to a world unimagined and without end?

My adventures in Koreatown will be on hiatus while I explore sidewalks three thousand miles south with the man I think I might marry, and with friends who have known me since the time I drove a VW bus and smoked a lot of funny cigarettes.

It's been years since I have been on a long meandering trip with no real itinerary outside of this country. The last time I did a trip like that, I was twenty-four. A nearly four-years long relationship had just ended and a new relationship was unfolding, and the latter was something unlike anything I'd ever experienced (what does that really mean? It means I was so in love and so full of deep and utter respect for this person; that when I visited his treehouse I fell in love with the slight scent of mold and when I saw him ride his bike or walk up to me on the street I wanted to cry and pull my hair out and yell my joy; that when he and I began to spend time with one another I felt fortunate, golden, and crazily brand-new...). The trip had been planned somewhere in the midst of the break-up and the developing love story. There was some minor twisting and turning about whether the ex might show up to meet me, without my knowledge, in Mexico. He hinted as much. He never showed. Instead, I left this country with an overnight-mailed audio -tape of music my new sweetheart put together for me. Instead, I landed in Mexico City and found my way to Guanajuato, then to San Miguel de Allende, then to Oaxaca, then Acapulco and back to Mexico City in a little under one month. Alone, with a backpack, a travel guide, and calling card with which I could make phone calls to the man who'd sent me the tape.

My talismans for the journey became the certain song by Bjork on the tape, which I played incessantly as the second-class buses motored me around Mexico; the biography of Georgia

O'Keeffe, which I found somewhere and read over the course of my trip; my black watchcap, which I wore to warm and protect my wet head as I walked every morning; and yes, the calling card, which connected me to this strange new person I was getting to know back home. I did fifty push-ups every morning in the pink bedroom I lived in for two weeks. It had two beds and two crucifixes. My subsequent bedrooms invariably had white walls and firm beds, turquoise walls and screenless windows, or modernist furniture and ocean views.

This particular voyage will include my current sweetheart and the same backpack I used for the trip to Mexico (the backpack was also strapped to said sweetheart as he traveled Guatemala two years ago). I've considered rereading the Georgia O'Keeffe biography on this trip but know that it will sting if I lose it. I prefer to bring along things I don't mind losing to the void. Except for my shoes. My expensive shoes are going to Ecuador. There is a wedding, after all.

◆

Ecuador
2 pairs of Dansko shoes: green sandals, black sandals.
2 shawls.
1 wool cap with ear flaps for the eternally cold grandmother.
1 bagful of finger puppets.
1 pink pig finger puppet.
1 unworn pair of black slacks.
6 packets of photos.
1 bathing suit requiring a wash.
3 handmade cards.
1 blue handbag.
1 roll of film yet to be developed.
3 packets of tea, never used.
1 tube of sunscreen.
4 lens wipes.
2 passports.
2 twenties.

1 dollar bill.
4 pairs of earrings from the coast.
1 dollar coin.
2 airplanes.
1 necklace from the coast.
3 voicemails.
5 hours of sleep.
1 stop for fuel in Panama.
26 emails.
19 hours awake.
2 of us who desperately missed our
2 cats.

SEVENTY-EIGHT

Súa, Ecuador

The bottom of my beer is making a great big puddle. Lady Youth is taking a swim in her yellow plastic goggles and breathing apparatus. Lord Fire & Play sits next to me, slumped in his chair while a tropical Madonna song plays, the one I danced to as a teenager with mi madre, the Goddess of Lonesome Debauchery. Lord F & P's eyelids move a little and his hands are folded over his recently acquired belly. I record the events and our surroundings as I am meant to, being Queen Opposition Sun and Moon. The plastic is sticky over the yellow tablecloth and the flies are monotonous, searching, alighting, looking for something we cannot give them. A mother goddess lounges nearby, watching Lady Youth in the water as her bikini shrinks evermore in the sea. My one hand is cramped from the record-keeping and the other is possessed by the swatting of flies, keeping them out of my carbonated nectar. The mother goddess watches dimly the vision of her husband in the water assisting, no—teaching—no, telling Lady Youth just how to use her goggles and breathing apparatus.

Grandfather Sol was out here earlier, his head slumped into his chest, until Negro the dog wandered by and he awoke and called him over. Witness the powerlessness lilting off the Grandfather's body, sliding away from his fingers and down the gritty cement to the sand and into the ocean. We are the guests of Grandfather Sol, but only we can hear the loud music raining down, en ingles y espanol. We are guests in the castle. I continue my recordings even if they are meant for no other eyes but my own, a greenish cast over the sky, a whale singing off in the distance to no one.

◆

Quito, Ecuador

In a gringo coffee shop near our hostel. Someone nearby freely saying fuck and sporting multiple facial piercings and talking of buying brandy and partying. S. is growling happily over the espresso just served to him and I have yet to sip my coffee. We are in a shaded area and there is the sound of people talking, the waiters calling out orders, horns honking, motors purring and clinking of glasses and coffee cups. I'm sucking on a Ricola and getting ready to pour a cold glass of water.

When I blow my nose each morning, there is a little tiny sprinkle of blood. We definitely overdid it yesterday despite our best intentions. S. thinks we walked four or five miles total. We pretty much overlooked all the cautions to take it easy the first few days, stay tranquilo, abstain from alcohol, drink lots of water. In fact, we did none of these things.

We chose the perfect time to visit the Teleferiqo. We all met in the lobby of the hostal at 4ish and rode a cab together that wound in and out of neighborhoods I had not yet seen in the three weeks we were in and out of Quito. Once at our stop, there was still an uphill walk and then a series of escalators, until we finally reached the line to enter the small cable cars that would carry us to the peak. When we left, the sun was out, preparing to set. After a short and very slow hike (due to the high altitude) with tremendous views of the surrounding volcanoes and clouds that looked within reaching distance of our arms if we stood underneath them, and after a glass of hot wine and a plate of cheeses and meats and vegetables, we rode back down the single cable, this time with no sunlight, and only the immense twinkling of Quito's lights down below us.

This is what my mind has felt like lately: the way my body feels when I'm driving on the freeway, fast, with the window open and my hair flailing about my face, the music loud and pounding and hypnotically melodic. Only right now it's all between my ears, this feeling.

SEVENTY-NINE

::I've put a number of books on hold at the library in one of my hold sprees. The majority deal with the issue of ecopsychology. This has been spurred by the number of times I hear the references to levees breaking in the media, and from there I jump to the Led Zeppelin rendition of the blues song "When the Levee Breaks," and from there I jump to the metaphor of levees breaking. When a levee broke a second time this weekend, the information seemed less like code and more like a straight-out S.O.S. of something that if you hadn't already picked up, was now screaming for attention.

::I just reread a Nancy Drew book that I have had since March 3, 1984 and it was one of the most entertaining books I have read in the last decade.

::I'm formulating an essay on my musical identity. This was spurred by 1) Andy asking me at K. and C.'s wedding who my absolute favorite musical artist is, and the hilarity that ensued (at my expense, really—but I'm used to that); 2) living with a music whore and dj who I watched dance in ecstasy the other night to the Waco Brothers live; 3) talking to K. and C. in Quito, Ecuador, over pizza, about my apparent lack of a musical identity; 4) buying tickets to see Dead Can Dance at the Hollywood Bowl, and realizing that this is an emotional purchase, with a specific purpose in its design, 5) the bubbling over of this and other things such as responses to music recently that have made me more attuned to what is going on in my head when some particular thing begins to play. Or not play.

::I'm finding threads that weave together from my dreams.

◆

Perhaps because when you spend three weeks anywhere new and different, you will peel off the experience like a skin and wear it around yourself. Little things remind me. The bumpy, pockmarked road reminds me of the taxi ride from Esmeraldas to Súa after the six hour descent on the curvy, two-lane Panamericana. Music blasting from cars driving in and out of Koreatown remind me of the three or four songs we heard over and over again in earnest throughout Quito, Atacames, Súa, and even the wedding: reggaeton, reggaeton, reggaeton. Tiny tiendas in my neighborhood make me think of buying a mosquito net in Atacames, and then frantically searching for something suitable to tie it down with (blue shoelaces). The Cuban restaurant on Virgil reminds me of fried plantains, the platacones we had with every meal by the equatorial waters. The turning of the season makes me wish for a fireplace like we had at Hacienda Cusin, when I realized that a fireplace could easily take the place of a television for me, a different story dancing every night.

It has now been three weeks since the three weeks spent in Ecuador. I miss the green bedspread and blue walls of the hostal by the ocean, the plastic patio furniture covered with the sand I brought in and out of the water with me, the 75 cent beers, the cobblestone streets, the innumerable trolleys, the piercing blue sky, the volcanoes, the daredevil bus and taxi drivers, the internet cafes, the sound of Andean flutes, the moody clouds, the hours laid out before us with time for reading, staring, swimming, playing ("¿eres tu my novia?"), writing, napping, eating, thinking.

EIGHTY

After listening to way too many sound bytes and replays of Resident Bush's speech yesterday, I realized that if different words were inserted, it would make an altogether different, more logical and more appropriate speech than the one we were subjected to.

I decided to have my way with it.

[Legend: all words in ( ) are my changes. Ellipses indicate where I cut paragraphs or words.]

All these separate images of destruction and suffering that we see on the news can seem like random and isolated acts of madness; innocent men and women and children have died simply because they boarded the wrong train, or worked in the wrong building, or checked into the wrong hotel. Yet while the killers choose their victims indiscriminately, their attacks serve a clear and focused ideology, a set of beliefs and goals that are evil, but not insane.

Some call this evil (capitalism); others, (imperialism); still others, (fascism). Whatever it's called, this ideology is very different from (true democracy). This form of radicalism exploits (the people of the U.S.) to serve a violent, political vision: the establishment, by terrorism and subversion and insurgency, of a totalitarian empire that denies all political and religious freedom. These extremists distort the idea of (democracy) into a call for terrorist murder against (anyone who doesn't agree with capitalism or U.S. imperialist policy).

Many militants are part of global, borderless terrorist organizations like (the CIA), which spreads propaganda, and provides financing and technical assistance to local extremists, and conducts dramatic and brutal operations like September the 11th...(The CIA) is more like a loose network with many branches than an army under a single command. Yet these operatives, fighting on scattered battlefields, share a similar ideology and vision for our world...

... Over the past few decades, (the U.S. has) specifically targeted Egypt, and Saudi Arabia, and Pakistan, and Jordan for potential takeover. They achieved their goal, for a time, in Afghanistan. Now (the U.S. government has) set...sights on Iraq... And we must recognize (the U.S.) as the central front in our war on terror...

... Evil men, obsessed with ambition and unburdened by conscience, must be taken very seriously—and we must stop them before their crimes can multiply.

Defeating the (imperialist) network is difficult, because it thrives, like a parasite, on the suffering and frustration of others. The (imperialists and capitalists) exploit local conflicts to build a culture of victimization, in which someone else is always to blame and violence is always the solution. They exploit resentful and disillusioned young men and women, recruiting them through (high school campuses, primarily in areas with high concentrations of youth of color) as the pawns of terror. And they exploit modern technology to multiply their destructive power...

The influence of (imperialism) is also magnified by helpers and enablers. They have been sheltered by authoritarian regimes, allies of convenience like (England), that share the goal of hurting (governments that don't agree with our imperialist stance)... These radicals depend on front operations, such as corrupted charities, which direct money to terrorist activity. They're strengthened by those who aggressively fund the spread of radical, intolerant versions of (Christianity) in unstable parts of the world. The militants are aided, as well, by elements of the (corporate) news media that incite hatred and (racism), that feed conspiracy theories and speak of a so-called (al Qaeda plot)...

... We're facing a radical (capitalist) ideology with inalterable objectives: to enslave whole nations and intimidate the world. No act of ours invited the rage of the killers—and no concession, bribe, or act of appeasement would change or limit their plans for murder.

On the contrary: (The U.S.) target(s) nations whose behavior they believe they can change through violence. Against such an enemy, there is only one effective response: (Peace and social justice movements) will never back down, never give in, and never accept anything less than complete victory. (*Applause.*)

The murderous ideology of the (radical Christian right) is the great challenge of our new century... Like the ideology of (capitalism), (the radical Christian right) is elitist, led by a self-appointed vanguard that presumes to speak for the (Christian) masses. (George W. Bush) says his own role is to tell (Christians)... "what is good for them and what is not." And what this man who grew up in wealth and privilege considers good for poor (Americans) is that they become killers and (soldiers). He assures them that his—that this is the road to paradise—though he never offers to go along for the ride.

Like the ideology of (the radical Christian right), our enemy teaches that innocent individuals can be sacrificed to serve a political vision. And this explains their cold-blooded contempt for human life. We've seen it in the murders of (countless Iraqi and American soldiers)
...When 25 Iraqi children are killed in a bombing, or Iraqi teachers are executed at their school, or hospital workers are killed caring for the wounded, this is murder, pure and simple—the total rejection of justice and honor and morality and religion...

...our... enemy pursues totalitarian aims. (U.S.) leaders pretend to be an aggrieved party, representing the powerless against (non-white) enemies. In truth (U.S. leaders) have endless ambitions of imperial domination, and they wish to make everyone powerless except themselves. Under their rule, they have banned books, and desecrated historical monuments, and brutalized women. They seek to end dissent in every form, and to control every aspect of life, and to rule the soul, itself. While promising a future of justice and holiness, the (U.S. government is) preparing for a future of oppression and misery...

And (capitalist and imperialist ideology)... contain inherent contradictions that doom it to failure. By fearing freedom—by distrusting human creativity, and punishing change, and limiting the contributions of half the population—this ideology undermines the very qualities that make human progress possible, and human societies successful. The only thing modern about the (capitalists') *vision is the weapons they want to use against us. The rest of their grim vision is defined by a warped image of the past—a declaration of war on the idea of progress, itself. And whatever lies ahead in the war against this ideology, the outcome is not in doubt: Those who despise freedom and progress have condemned themselves to isolation, decline, and collapse. Because free peoples believe in the future, free peoples will own the future. (Applause.)*

We didn't ask for this global struggle, but we're answering history's call with confidence, and a comprehensive strategy. Defeating a broad and adaptive (imperialist) network requires patience, constant pressure, and strong partners (all over the world from your neighborhood and beyond). Working with these partners, we're disrupting militant conspiracies, destroying their ability to make war, and working to give millions in a troubled region of the world a hopeful alternative to resentment and violence…

…Our commitment is clear: We will not relent until the organized international terror networks are exposed and broken, and their leaders held to account for their acts of murder…

Any government that chooses to be an ally of terror has also chosen to be an enemy of civilization. And the (peace-loving) world must hold those (imperialist) regimes to account…

The (imperialists) are as brutal an enemy as we've ever faced. They're unconstrained by any notion of our common humanity...

There's always a temptation, in the middle of a long struggle, to seek the quiet life, to escape the duties and problems of the world, and to hope the enemy grows weary of fanaticism and tired of murder. This would be a pleasant world, but it's not the world we live in. The (imperialist) is never tired, never sated, never content with yesterday's brutality. This enemy considers every retreat of the civilized world as an invitation to greater violence…

…We're standing with dissidents and exiles against oppressive regimes, because we know that the dissidents of today will be (part of the solution) tomorrow…

…With the rise of a deadly enemy and the unfolding of a global ideological struggle, our time in history will be remembered for

new challenges and unprecedented dangers. And yet the fight we have
joined is also the current expression of an ancient struggle, between
those who put their faith in dictators, and those who put their faith
in the people. Throughout history, tyrants and would-be tyrants have
always claimed that murder is justified to serve their grand vision—
and they end up alienating decent people across the globe. Tyrants
and would-be tyrants have always claimed that regimented societies
are strong and pure—until those societies collapse in corruption and
decay. Tyrants and would-be tyrants have always claimed that free
men and women are weak and decadent—until the day that free men
and women defeat them . . .

◆

Many conversations this weekend spun around where we might one day end up living. Pros and cons flitted and floated about the Bay Area vs. Los Angeles. It's a tough call in some ways [and in other ways, not]. We're committed to being where we believe we're most needed, our politics rearing their beautiful heads as we say this aloud and volley it about, trying it on, wondering at it and how far this line of thought will lead us. [I'm going to change the phrase "the palpable struggle" now to just saying that] the struggle, here, is palpable. We're fighting sweatshops and shitty educational systems, AIDS, and racism in our everyday lives. [Still, always trying to weave in the "for" and decrease the "anti-."] I remember when I wanted to get a black band tattooed on my upper arm [Bush had been positioned in office the first time and I wanted to show my anti-status, forever, on my arm]. Always outside of something. Always yelling for change. Now, I wish to remember all that I am in alignment with, and yes, some of those things can be found in a 500 mile move north—but in the end, it feels too far away from the desert and the warm coastline I love, that I feel rooted to.

When we start speaking in temporaries, I can envision it.

EIGHTY-ONE

Santa Cruz

The long curvy roads massage us out to the place called downtown. My eyes and heart are reminded of Olympia. I have been here one night, and spent it in a bar with AQ and her cohort. My eyes and heart are reminded of when I flew to Spokane to be with J. as he started his MFA program, the dark bar he took me to, our pretending that we were just friends, and we were, but we liked to have sex in front of his fireplace, too, and my boyfriend knew this and drove me to the airport anyway. Twice. So once again, I am in a dark bar where smoke is outlawed and we are swathed in smoke and surrounded by PhD students. I imbibe conversations and Sierra Nevadas. My dollar bills are fed to and ingested by an internet jukebox machine, and I play a little "Crimson and Clover" and send a sweet nothing down south to my sweetie. AQ plays Nick Cave and last call finds us tipping our glasses back in surprise that we made it to last call.

Vegan menu items and a sign that reads "Do not Hump." Girlie girls saunter in and then freak out laughing and scurry back out. Hot chocolate soothes and prepares our way home. On the road: two deer. We slow and for the third or fourth time I am amazed, loudly, that we are so close to the Mystery Spot. At 4am we are ready to shoot out the lights back at the end of the curvy road. And we do.

The night is dark. Theda is sitting guard on the front step. Bean is curled on the couch. I sip and flirt with the red wine after a day of coffee, an afternoon of sinking into a notebook and a binder full of articles and work by other writers that I am finally able to get a fix on. I throw a lot of the papers away until the binder is slim and holds only the most pressing matters between its covers. We see Nicole, a woman who is studying uniforms. Okay, it's not that simple, but I like the sound of it. I take notes and finally begin the tome weighing my bag down. Delicious Vollmann, raining down on me in this dry autumn wind. In less than an hour we'll travel that squirrely road back to town. My body keeps asking me when it's time to fall back to the bed, sleep.

I leave this afternoon. I've been dipping deeply into William T. Vollmann and writing: new work, lists, letters to friends. Time like this makes me remember that staying with someone always results in inspiration. I'm inspired to be much more disciplined about my writing; inspired to never turn the television on again; inspired to find the woods; inspired to enjoy the moments more fully when I come away from the writing. The days have been segmented into long bouts of reading, running, writing, then a coming together for dinner, with wine and conversations bubbling before returning home again, the curvy road back into the woods and back into our separate rooms to return to the work.

This week was "Sex Week" on a local news station. Historically I have been in love with three people born this week. It was the week of Scorpio's end with a full moon in Taurus: exactly opposite my natal sun and moon. It was the week of my half-birthday.

•

Yesterday I soared through seven miles in Griffith Park and through parts of Burbank. I renegaded by abandoning my group, going it alone. I had my thoughts, fantasies, and the warm winds. These are the days when I love Southern California so much my skin tingles—the sky a deep blue; the sun baking us lightly; the hills and mountains like brown suede so that I wish I could touch them, brush my cheek against their flanks; the palm trees rustling and waving at all of us down below at their knotty trunks that look like elephant legs. I want to capture the warm air and hug it against me. Autumn breathes underneath it all despite the warmish temperature and the Santa Ana winds. In my creative writing class this week, I asked the boys I teach to use all of their senses to describe the Santa Ana winds that were hurtling, furying, slapping and rushing outside. I walked to the door and flung it open for them. We could hear the full volume of it and their faces lit up and they bent to write with a different kind of energy than usual. I had told them of Joan Didion's essay about the Santa Anas, and I had mentioned the full moon. One of them called the winds "Santana." Each piece they read aloud mentioned both the wind and the full moon and every last piece was thick with metaphor, purpose and a sense of wildness. It reminded me of all the effort it takes to channel energies effectively, appropriately. And how this week is one of those weeks when the effort takes more concentration, more intention, and that dose of wildness I need to make it through without combusting.

Tomorrow we leave for a plot of ten acres in the desert near Phoenix, Arizona.

After much too much cajoling, I got one of my running mates to meet me in Marina del Rey on Saturday morning, where we planned to join up with fellow marathoners for a fresh landscape—twenty miles of fresh landscape. I told myself I'd love it because it would be different than the trails and paths of Griffith Park, Glendale and Burbank that I've been tramping up and down on since September, and that I'd also love it because it would be by the ocean. Twenty miles is twenty miles, though. I have never run up and down the Venice Boardwalk like that and maybe will never again, nor had I ever started in MDR and gone past the Santa Monica Pier, nor had I ever pushed past the Palisades on foot and descended into Brentwood, only to turn around and head back on trails I walked a year ago at this time when I was a catsitter by the beach.

•

Today I got the news that a person in my regular Sunday marathon group—not my pace group, but the larger group that meets on Sundays before splitting into pace groups—collapsed yesterday on our Griffith Park run. She died hours later of cardiac arrest. She was 22. She was ten miles into the twenty-mile run.

The pain in my tendon running down into my right foot,

which had to be taped up the night before the run, which hurts like hell when I first step on it in the morning, every morning, suddenly seems small and inconsequential—not in a way that means I won't care for it, but in a way that simply puts things into some type of perspective I'm still sorting out.

The last two weeks have been all about perspective, and being willing to look past the tasks in my hands, being thrown to my hands, falling out of my hands, to see something grander— like seeing the black sky behind the full moon.

The feeling takes me back to sitting on the overstuffed couch watching a small girl's face go from stone still to warm and buttery—those first several minutes after she had emerged from her nap. Her eyes looked focused on something perpetually far away, and there was time spent curled in on herself not answering any questions until she was ready, even, to listen. This is the feeling I have, I who never take naps during the day, having just taken one, immediately prior having created a collage (images of flower headdress, red carnation burlesque, green seeds taking root, maps flat with red paths drawn in squiggles across their terrain). The effort pulled the string right out of me. I had to curl in, gestate on the couch.

EIGHTY-TWO

I have used screwdrivers, corkscrews, sheer strength and will surging up and down my legs in cold wind, my mouth, mixing spoon and chopping utensil, slow cooker and sponge, paste and scissors, heart and counsel. These are evenings of friends visiting all at once in my living room, orange and green candles burning spice scents in the air, intricately wrapped presents with ribbons coming undone in my hands, small white lights on a tree that still thinks to live while a cat drinks from its red planter. The cacti in the house are happy with the attention paid them. The heater gets lit when it has to and the warm fuzzy blue bathrobe may even stow away for the night ride in our welcoming bed as firecrackers sizzle and burst in the sky.

I shiver and my teeth chatter. I wake up hot with covers thrown off and a cat resting in the crook of my neck. Her fur is my cape and her breathing is all I hear. I wait several minutes, looking into the ceiling. The cracks on the wall. The walls we will paint before the new year, the bookcases that need to be bought (you know you're a nerd when you excitedly talk bookcases, and how big they come, I've been told this week), the old crinkled green money that will be mine to spend as I see fit on something just for me. Massage, journal, subscription? Donation, appetizers and wine? Savings or checking? It is better to just lay here underneath all the questions, yawn, imagine the next seven days of open-endedness.

I remind myself of the pact and all it will take to ensure the sanctity of it is a little paragraph here and a little paragraph there. I've told the idea of the story out loud to at least two people now: one with an advanced degree in psychology and one who will have her second book of fiction published next year. I trace my index finger on the gray Formica and wait for the story to wash over like a river across the length of me. Little spiny pieces come:

tossed image here, bucket of language there. The pens, which I've come to rely on, having nothing to do with it after all.

♦

We thought we would find it behind this door, but we did not.

Sunday, after my eight-mile run, we drove the 156-odd miles to the desert, our first trip out there this year. Number 10 gave us heartburn and bad dreams, lumpy pillows and a whirring heater that had to stay on all night.

It was elsewhere that we found what we wanted. Two things. No, three things.

We were bundled up against the wind, walking in the dust towards an adobe bungalow we could open up a door to and peek at. We'd breakfasted at Country Kitchen and touched tools of the trade for rock climbing, pulled on doors to places that were closed for the holiday, and driven around beach ball-sized tumbleweeds. We were on the verge of finding what we'd been looking for.

When I had imagined a ceremony in the desert, I had imagined the necessity of water. I could envision my bare feet in sand, the wind low and whistling, the moon whole.

Then, behind the bungalows: this. I'd wondered where the water would come from—a fountain? A ritual spilling on the sand? This oasis found us.

A pomegranate tree.

We had turned a half-moon around the oasis and found ourselves underneath this beauty, parched and dry in the winter sun. As soon as he took my wrists in his hands and looked me in the eye, I knew.

Twenty-six miles traversed by foot and the next day, a trip to the desert. Palm Springs sublime. The corridor to Yucca Valley. The little boy version of the man I know growing up somewhere in this stretch: not even he knows where exactly (then Barstow, then McAllister, Oklahoma, thus establishing him as a self-proclaimed Okie). Past the Water Canyon Coffee Company and up the road, framed by clouds. Dips and upward dives in the pavement and a slow turning off onto dust road. We are again in

133

number 10. Fake fireplace and working heater. Kitchenette and tea kettle. Cactus and quilts. We make our way to Pappy Hour and arrive just a little too late, though not so late that we miss Victoria Williams and the rest of the gorgeous Thrift Store All Star Band who we are beginning to crush out on. "Please Don't Be Long" by the Beatles and I wonder if they mean *please don't be long or please don't belong.* I fit either way. Stellas, golden and cold. Steak dinner, split plate. We awake again at 3am to read by lamplight. The next day, we write our postcards: please see us get married next year at the full moon and lunar eclipse. My fingers falter just a little, because this clinches it: I'm getting hitched, all right. Yep. Come see. I'll be the one wearing orange like the desert mariposa. He'll be the one in the nudie suit, embroidered with renditions of the flowers we held between our fingertips, never severing them from their stems.

EIGHTY-THREE

The Valley

My sandaled feet stepped around and over gravemarkers and once I almost tripped into a hole in the grass designed to hold flowers. We arrived late, but not late enough that we missed poems being read (Walt Whitman, Joy Harjo, and Thich Nat Hanh). The sun was beating down on us just two days after rain pounded the concrete and this place of wide acres of grass, and stone, and statues. I kept looking at the very deep pink of one of her cheeks, and the way her chin puckered.

I don't know the customs of funerals. I barely know the wedding ceremony and keep seeing it done in probably the most radical, beautiful ways possible. The ceremony I witnessed today was equally beautiful, replete with religious prayer and symbol and movement, and I notice that I am old enough to not feel a need to rebel against it the way I did in high school, but to let it envelope me, pass through.

I can be so messy. Tears, runny nose, sweat, parched lips. I am not compact or easy or straight; I am skilled at closing up, turning out the light, pulling down the shade—but only manage to sometimes. I cried under the sun behind my big brown sunglasses. I listened to the religious prayer and chant and even wished I had something of my own like that. I thought of the bond between mother and child that I resist in my own life, wanting to believe it's not that big of a deal when everything else in the culture—and my experience—says the opposite. I thought of mentorship and its many incarnations, how the bereaved is someone I regularly observe, learn from, model my behavior on, and also someone whom I admire, care for, and laugh with. Her pink cheek. Her puckered chin.

Afterwards, there were sandwiches, vegetables, and coffee. I met new people and felt the common thread in the room.

I was a piece of it: not some little knot, but an offshoot thread that belonged.

•

Spent several days of the last week in Austin, Texas. We flew over El Paso where my grandmother was born and raised. I walked across a bridge several times, not knowing it was the bridge that the bats live under. At night they fly out from underneath, darkening the sky. Most nights I was sipping free drinks at various parties and missed the bat show. It wasn't until Sunday morning, when I took a four-mile walk/run along the river, that I read the kiosk signs alerting me to the bats and their temporary home. You can get a box from the bat conservation folks, or make your own, to help house the bats, and the kiosk featured photos of six or so little bats huddled into the safety of the wood. It made me wish I lived in Austin. The row of bars and tattoo shops also made me wish I lived in Austin. The slap of thick, wet air didn't. I promised my love we'd go to Austin next year around the same time, and it might be what some would term, 'the honeymoon.'

•

The marathon is a week over. I thought of it fondly last night as I threw back the umpteenth Stella in the darkness of Pappy & Harriet's and listened to the low, tumultous sounds of Bartender's Bible. A week to the day I'd been running and walking and stumbling and shuffling down the closed streets of Los Angeles, and what a way to see the city...at times apocalyptic, as though this was the L.A. post-bomb, when thoroughfares like Crenshaw or Wilshire were emptied of cars and we could make our way down the middles like zippers closing up the city, with orange rinds, banana peels and crushed cups underneath our shoes.

As we drove out of the city on Saturday afternoon towards the desert, we were greeted by thousands upon thousands of people marching for immigrant rights in the streets of Los Angeles. They stood on the freeway overpasses of the 101 and we honked, waved, and struck our fists in the air, our solidarity on the move. It was utterly amazing. I've been a part of some big protests, but this wave of people was something unlike anything I'd ever seen. My favorite sign: *you bug us so much you've awakened the Sleeping Giant.* While we weren't on the streets, our spirits were, just as they are today with every student participating in a walkout.

And then: the desert. We wound our way around as we always do on these monthly sojourns that make the land, and its landmarks, all the more familiar to us. I love getting up to the spot where the cell phone loses all connection, and there is no sound but the wind. We pass under the wooden gate and create a different home away from home.

♦

C. just left the apartment a little while ago from having done a photo shoot. I'm not sure how many times I've been the subject, but it seems like a lot. I feel as though the first photos she ever took of me were of my first tattoo, close up, so that you could see every black curve and swirl. Today the subjects were my 'text tattoos' for her first solo show in New York. She set up from suitcases and folded tripods and 99 cent store containers a little studio in my bedroom, and we moved the dresser to reveal enough cat hair for another cat altogether, and the one white wall good enough for a shoot in the entire apartment.

C. was shooting some special Polaroid type film and she hid herself underneath a black cape much like you see in old-time movies of photographers. It's important to stay perfectly still, because the tripod moves ever so little, and so does the subject. When one is asked to stand still, it's amazing how the body still succumbs to the little tugs and pulls in the air, the breaths moving the body millimeters forward or backward.

The cat slept on the bed, her eyes closed and she in her egg-laying position, moving slightly only whenever the flash popped. A chilly wind blew in from the open window so that goosebumps populated my skin. The photos came out wonderfully regardless.

The smaller-than-a-postage-stamp photo is from a shoot

137

C. did with me and S., when we were not even dating yet. I was dating Sh., who, when he heard about a dream I had about S., suggested it might mean S. was actually my "soulmate." After he suggested this, he pushed me back onto the grass at Griffith Park and asked me if I wanted to hump.

There is S.'s hand, and there is my long hair.

EIGHTY-FOUR

::ingredients for resuscitation::
*one teaspoon basil
*one warm bath, drawn at sunset
*one bar of apricot & fig soap, fresh
*open window
*tears from liquid brown eyes
*1/4 herbed cookie
*one mindbending evening
*one massage for 75 minutes by a woman with a mysteriously lovely accent and clear braces in her teeth
*small orange candles
*foot lotion from Sarah's post-marathon care package
*green tea rejuvenating face mask
*Six Feet Under
*black bean soup
*two cats with liquid green eyes
*sunlight
*peppermint tea
*6 minutes, 4 immersions in bath water
*when necessary, only when absolutely necessary, acetaminophen
*daydreaming on the couch in the place he thinks of as their "lodge"
*reading of six library books at a time

EIGHTY-FIVE

Joshua Tree

I'm on Sunkist Road, sitting outside, listening to the fountain and the small thunder of the water heater, and S. is making French toast and bacon, and I'm in a tank top and pajama pants, writing, coffeeing. The colors, everywhere, are alarmingly sharp and beautiful. The palm tree in front of me is thorny, fanned, perfect. We are the only ones here: I am 98% sure of this. We arrived yesterday, ate mole enchiladas. Our hostess was kind, with her marvelously clear skin and hazel eyes. She exuded more than the usual warmth and friendliness. Her husband was at the bungalows. We discovered him there, gardening. We fell in love with the place again, and it just got more and more magnified, this love.

After her husband left, we smoked out on the private patio and commenced to wandering. I spent some time alone in the garden area and enjoyed looking at practically every square inch of trees and cacti, and the pond, surrounded by things like a ceramic rooster, and a flamingo, and broken coffee mugs, and there were many anthills to admire, and hummingbirds and big fat black bees, and the sky was very dramatic, gray and cloudy and then patches of blue. One tree had loads of little yellow buds on it like pom poms. Another tree had what looked like a little muff of leaves at its trunk. Everything, while expertly landscaped, looked wonderously wild, still.

S. went over to the ranch down the road, and we walked down there together after awhile, after the sun set. The sand on the road was pure white, and soft. The entrance to the ranch and its fencing was made up of branches, the sign painted expertly, so that the name of the ranch was made up of a cursive of illustrated ropes. On our way back, we were shocked at how the mountains stood out, their backdrop the violet lighting of the city.

Later, I took S. to the parts of the property I'd wandered, and we walked over to where the tumbleweed are made of barbed wire, and peered into a dark shell of metal surrounded by goat droppings. We ventured into the other patios that we could access, since we were becoming increasingly certain that we were the only ones there. My favorite patio housed many statuettes of deer in various poses, and a little bull on a wagon wheel.

For dinner, S. made chicken breasts stuffed with cheese, sundried tomatoes and basil, asparagus and peas, and a simple pasta with butter and fresh herbs. Afterwards, we sat outside in the shared patio. The lights were solar-powered, or on a timer, and softly popped on when the sky was very dark. Patsy Montana crooned from the stereo. S. tried to yodel until we lost our breath laughing. Later that night, after I plunged into the soft bed and burrowed under the covers, I dreamt I had the lucky 13 tattooed on my lower arm, underneath, where the skin is palest on my body. In the dream, I was slightly aghast, since the numbers were huge and beautifully done, with shading and flames, all in black. It had chosen me, so I was bound to wear it. I woke up the next morning, and here I sit, contemplating the luck of the draw, this place, this color and light, and this coffee, so achingly perfect and the vision of what we will create in this place less than a year from now, when we wed.

◆

I rolled double 3s on Tuesday. Last week, I took the hike that became such an integral part of my existence back when I lived in Los Feliz. It seemed right to return. Up into the fog I went. I came across one man I remembered from back then, and he was wearing gold chains and a sweatband, and he was grinning and friendly as usual. He remembered me. "I come here everyday. I go up twice," he said. Twice? I asked. "Yes, better than a gym," he said. As I ran down the hill, I considered that he was absolutely spot-on.

I met the other man of wisdom today as I trekked up. I'd wondered when I would encounter him, if I would encounter him. He was barefoot, holding his shoes, coming down the dirt path. "Long time, no see," he said. My right hand gave my left hand the car keys I'd been grasping (no pockets today) and he lifted his arm as I lifted mine. SMACK. SMACK. SMACK. "You so strong!" he bellowed.

I walked forward and I walked backward. I ran and I trotted. I smiled and said hello, good morning, and buenos dias. I twirled an ankle, stretched a calf and took deep breaths. Welcome to the double 3s.

EIGHTY-SIX

::(short) visit to the deep::

    Our conversations seem to dip right into the deep end. She tells me that the night before, she went to a rancho, where she was crowned queen of...queen of... "I can't remember," she states, finally, and because earlier she mentioned something about a Cadillac (then forgot what she was talking about), I offer, "Queen of the Cadillacs?" She shakes her head.

    Sometimes I am her sister; other times I'm her sobrina. Often she does not remember my name. The first time we visited her, she seemed to clue in only to me, as though discarding her daughter completely, which is, in effect, what my mother has been used to all her life from this woman. The thought that I would become the only person my grandmother might ever recognize again was overwhelming—I felt shot up with metal, my blood becoming thin and silver, and a drowning feeling came over me.

    This was not to be after all. We are told that the name she hollers at night is my mother's. It's fitting, perhaps, that my mother's name translates to "sorrow" in English.

EIGHTY-SEVEN

Irvine Meadows

K. decided that we should start the concert season early, since our first tickets to the Hollywood Bowl don't get us there until July 30, so we were off to what used to be known as Irvine Meadows on a Friday evening to see Peaches, Bauhaus, and Nine Inch Nails.

I can't recall the last time I was at Irvine Meadows, and the recollections I do have involve lots of grass, and blankets, and people dancing in the night, drugs, a pack of girls that moved with me like an amoeba, and the parking lot that could be any parking lot I visited during those days, complete with nitrous balloons, colorful wayfarers, empty beer cans, and the glubglubglub of someone taking a royally huge bong hit. This, I knew, would be far different from this particular show. There was a hint of parking lot action, but I ate half a magic cookie and K. and I laughed our way to the entrance. We, being early and late thirties, got something called 'premiere parking' which made me feel strangely adult, but mostly just cost a lot of extra money for a shorter walk to the entrance.

Then: yes, nearly everyone was wearing some manifestation of black, or fishnet, or mesh, or leather or vinyl or petticoats or corset. Condoms were being given away like candy and people were scooping them up as such. We took the hike up to the unreserved lawn where we'd put down our blanket for the night. It was still light when Bauhaus took the stage (due to traffic, we missed Peaches. Sigh) and I could lay back on the blanket and still view Peter Murphy's performance broadcast over the three large screens above the stage.

K. and I went through a strong confusion, cookie-related, no doubt, but one that we didn't confide with each other about until halfway through NIN's set...who was that muscular pretty boy with the microphone? Why was his hair cut so short to the scalp? His voice was absolutely familiar, but... And it wasn't until we confided in each other this uncertainty that we realized it was indeed Mr. Reznor, but...wow. Who was this Trent Reznor, anyway? When not staring down the amazing light show and this cut, sexy man yelling and gasping and modulating his voice all over my eardrums, I was thoroughly entertained by the crowd. I wondered at the groups and clumps of people I saw and wondered: what is it that we have in common that we're all here tonight? The people right around us were not even familiar with Peaches or Bauhaus, so we were all in for NIN...but really, what is the connection? What is the collective unconscious drive to be, there, at that moment?

One of the most beautiful things that night, and maybe ever, was listening to the entire audience croon into the night: *You can have it all. My empire of dirt. I will let you down. I will make you hurt.*

•

White wine, oranges, and nectarines accompanied us to the Hollywood Bowl once again. When was the first time I saw Ozomatli? That is a mystery, and so is how many times, and if the last time really was back on New Year's Eve 2001 as we rolled into 2002, which proved to be one of the hardest years of my adult life (right after 2001).

The line-up took me right back to adolescence, as did the familiar Los Angeles chaparral we could see in the near distance—it took me back to the days of reggae fests at the Greek Theater, where we practically set up camp, a bunch of teenagers and I, with smuggled vodka in the car and frisbees and ponchos and intricate little pipes and Guatemalan print bags. We spent plenty of time in the parking lot, on the grass, and in the rows of vendors—sticky sweet incense, spicy pungent smoke, red, yellow, black and green—we liked to be in the thick of it.

Last night I was an adult with white wine and a corkscrew and the only bags we carried were a backpack and an all-purpose canvas bag filled with water and food. Our seats were in the very back, and I could not help but think that as a teenager, I would have loved that—there's a long corridor butting up against the dry brown hill with bushes, perfect for dancing, meeting new people, moseying along following the smoke. Instead, we sat in our seats and smoked, and I reminisced with two people older than I, both of whom I've known only in the last decade or so, total, about the fact that I began going to shows like this one when I was 15 years old. And here I am, 33, doing the same dance, maybe with less costly tickets (the irony—I have less money now than when I did when I was 15 and lived rent-free), and with 18 years between me and the first time I entered the throbbing throngs of a Reggae Sunsplash or a Bob Marley Festival.

We left early, metro'ing it home, and made one stop. We are 40, 38, and 33, and at 11:30 p.m. on a Sunday night when we all had to work the next day, we made each other laugh eating chocolate donuts at the 24-hour donut shop around the corner from the apartment. It made me happy to be an adult.

EIGHTY-EIGHT

Last night as I left Central Juvenile Hall after what felt like an especially successful teaching experience, I decided to forego the freeway. It would have been so easy—a short jaunt, the ribbon of asphalt that would take me next to City Hall and underneath overpasses so I could spy on downtown, speeding along with all the others towards the mid-city. Instead, I found myself turning right on Cesar Chavez, thinking of the times my mother and I have crossed the bridge on our way to pick up tamales and pan dulce, and crossing back over, sometimes from La Mascota, sometimes, long ago, from my grandmother's house.

       Cesar Chavez turned into Sunset and everyone on the road seemed lightly, magically calm—no speeders. The night was young and warm and nuzzled into my open window as I followed the curvy thread into Echo Park. It felt good. I thought of how I traded in life in a town of 30,000 people for a return to the metropolis, and I was pleased. I loved Sunset, I loved that I could turn left and my eyes could fill with Echo Park lake and its lotuses, and I could turn right on Temple and go past the police station, and when I came to a light and the opposite car was a black and white, I could keep singing the rusty old song coming out of the radio loud and strong, and think of the boys in juvenile hall, and how they had had to enter that place at the hands of the police, and how I felt compassion for the whole of the situation. Then there are all the places I've never been. The Tribal Cafe. The gallery where S. meets his co-conspirators. Elysian Park on a weekday where K. walks her dogs daily. And I love L.A. all the more . . .

EIGHTY-NINE

It was the last remaining concert we would go to that summer, and it ended on a cloggin'-worthy rendition of "I Saw the Light"*.

Today is my mother's birthday.

> *I wandered so aimless, life filled with sin*
> *I wouldn't let my dear saviour in*
> *Then Jesus came like a stranger in the night*
> *Praise the lord, I saw the light*

At the end of this month, a ten-year relationship will end.

> *I saw the light, I saw the light*
> *No more darkness, no more night*
> *Now I'm so happy, no sorrow in sight*
> *Praise the lord, I saw the light*

I'm at the six-month mark: six months until I marry a firecracker, the sputtering neon kind that whisks around at your feet wooing you with color. Watch out: hot (and this kind never fizzes out).

> *Just like a blind man I wandered along*
> *Worries and fears I claimed for my own*
> *Then like the blind man that god gave back his sight*
> *Praise the lord - I saw the light*

Possibly in the works: a radio show. A literary journal (yet again!). I return to (completely rewriting) the manuscript set aside four years ago.

I saw the light, I saw the light
No more darkness, no more night
Now I'm so happy, no sorrow in sight
Praise the lord, I saw the light

When I returned to my old hiking trail last week, the old man who likes to slap my hands and tell me how strong I am, as he's done for the last four years on the trail, asked "Do you have the spirit of God?"

I paused. "Mmm, yes," I said.

"Good! Good!" I didn't tell him I had the spirit, alright, my gods are plentiful. He asked me to read the small white piece of paper he held. Something about not needing the word in ink, but in the "fleshy tables of the heart," words both in English and Korean. I read the English. And I continued on down the hill.

I was a fool to wander and stray
Straight is the gate and narrow the way
Now I have traded the wrong for the right
Praise the lord, I saw the light

This manuscript may find another incarnation; it remains to be seen. It may move on over, it may fold up and fly away to become something else altogether (I lean towards the latter). That then, ends an almost three and a half year project. Until next time.

I saw the light, I saw the light
No more darkness, no more night
Now I'm so happy, no sorrow in sight
Praise the lord, I saw the light.

*lyrics by Hank Williams

NINETY

I am getting married. Hitched, ring on a finger.

Exhausted beyond belief.

Barely getting through a magazine, let alone Underworld, the book of the moment.

Sexual energy pulsing when I'd rather it not.

Stuck in a hotel room, alone, mostly, and a heated pool with a sky shrouded in fog. Too much red wine, not enough gentle people.

Sex charge rapid fire when she's in the room. Or my three foot radius. Or in the same building, one floor below.

I am getting married. Hitched, ring on a finger.

The moon appears for a moment before the fog shrouds her and I know how she feels.
I know. I know. I know.

Almost time to hibernate.

AUTHOR BIO

WENDY C. ORTIZ is the author of the critically acclaimed *Excavation: A Memoir* and the dreamoir *Bruja*. Her work has been featured in the *Los Angeles Times, the Los Angeles Review of Books*, and the National Book Critics Circle Small Press Spotlight blog. She is a psychotherapist in private practice in Los Angeles.

ACKNOWLEDGMENTS

My thanks to Writ Large Press + CCM for faith, time, love, and energy. Thank you, Karrie Higgins. Thank you, Sandy Lee. Gratitude to all the ghosts that inhabit this book.

OFFICIAL

CCM ●

GET OUT OF JAIL
* VOUCHER *

- -

Tear this out.
Skip that social event.
It's okay.
You don't have to go if you don't want to. Pick up
the book you just bought. Open to the first page.
You'll thank us by the third paragraph.

If friends ask why you were a no-show, show them
this voucher.
You'll be fine.

- -

We're coping.

●

Printed in October 2021
by Rotomail Italia S.p.A., Vignate (MI) - Italy